Science to Go

Science to Go

Fact and Fiction Learning Packs

Judy Sauerteig

2001
Libraries Unlimited, Inc.
Englewood, Colorado

Dedicated to
Clifford and Irene Thomas—
my mom and dad,
my educators—
and to Gary, Traci, and Abbie,
my education.

Libraries Unlimited, Inc.
P.O. Box 6633
Englewood, CO 80155-6633
1-800-237-6124
www.lu.com

Library of Congress Cataloging-in-Publication Data

Sauerteig, Judy.
   Science to go : fact and fiction learning packs / Judy Sauerteig.
     p. cm.
   Includes bibliographical references and index.
   ISBN 1-56308-844-4 (soft)
   1. Science--Study and teaching (Elementary)--Activity programs. I. Title.

LB1585 .S27 2001
372.3'5044--dc21

00-050704

Contents

Grade 2

Grade 3

Acknowledgments

I would like to thank:

- all the students and parents at Cherry Creek Academy for being so supportive of this project
- the staff at Cherry Creek Academy for their interest and support
- Sally Wallace for the initial inspiration
- Pat Jackson for allowing me to invade her classroom for two months
- Judy Bentley for making me laugh
- Barbara Simon, Maureen Dreman, Dorothy Raisio, and Beth Quinn for their beautiful artwork on the bags
- Marilyn Bowman, my sister, who listened patiently
- my family for their support and love

Introduction

These learning packs were developed for a variety of reasons, and during the development process a variety of uses were discovered. Initially an effort was made to provide materials for parents to work in depth with their students on specific curriculum topics to reinforce and support classroom studies. There are several important advantages. The learning packs provide yet another way for parents and children to read together. The concept of fiction and nonfiction is reinforced. The parents and students realize the enjoyment of reading nonfiction. The parents also either learn new material or refresh their memories. If students need a review of material due to absences, the books provide a new way to introduce and reinforce concepts taught in the classroom. Literacy awareness is also a benefit. New teachers in need of materials can use the learning packs in the classroom to present information.

Each book group contains one nonfiction book title, one related fiction book title, and an activity sheet based on the books. They can be organized to adapt to any situation: library, classroom, or home. The book bags have worked well. They are canvas bags, approximately 12-by-14-inches with a handle. Included in each bag is a paperback copy of each book, which keeps the cost down. The activity sheets and a parent information sheet (p. x) are enclosed in plastic sheet protectors. Also included is a small spiral notebook to be used as a journal if students or parents would like to add ideas or comment on the use of the books.

Managing the Book Bags

The bags can be displayed in many ways in the media center. I have chosen to hang them on a wall using a grid on which hooks have been placed. They are organized according to grade level and color coded for ease in reshelving.

The bags were decorated by a parent using markers specially made for use on cloth. I then sprayed them with Scotchgard™ to keep them as clean as possible. Yes, they will get dirty, but they are washable (they do shrink a little). Transfers might also be used, or art students could decorate the bags. The possibilities are endless.

Luggage tags work very well for application of a bar code. The clear, self-laminating tags fit around the handle and provide protection for easy access to the bar code.

The information sheet for parents (p. x) and the activity sheets are placed in clear protectors. If the activity sheet is to be written on, large storage bags can be used to accommodate multiple copies.

Information for Parents

Welcome to a fun way to help your student at home. These packets have several important objectives:

- to promote literacy

- to reinforce the Core Knowledge Curriculum Units

- to reinforce the importance of reading aloud with children

- to clarify and emphasize the difference between fiction and nonfiction

- to encourage nonfiction reading for enjoyment

- to extend and enrich lessons learned in the classroom

- to review lessons learned in the classroom

- to provide parents with some structured activities to assist students

Each packet includes two books, one fiction and one nonfiction, and an activity sheet for each. After reading the books aloud together, you may choose any or all of the activities depending on time and your own child. If the book sparks a discussion and that is all you have time for, that is wonderful. Please don't treat these like teacher-assigned homework.

Some of the activity sheets include information that may be of help to you. The grade and unit with which the books are integrated is indicated immediately following the heading.

One additional beneficial activity that supports the writing program would be to have your student write a summary of each of the books. A summary is a general statement of the theme of the book. It should be short and concise and not include details. A journal is provided for this activity, or the student may write about the experience of doing the packet. Comments are welcomed.

These activities are only suggestions and a springboard for any other ideas that may be formulated by student or parent. If you create successful activities and you would like to share them with others, please write them up in the journal and return it with the learning pack.

I hope you enjoy the books, activities, and special times with your student.
HAVE FUN!!!

Kindergarten

Apples

Plants and Plant Growth–K

TOPIC: APPLES

NONFICTION: *How Do Apples Grow?* by Betsy Maestro

FICTION: *The Seasons of Arnold's Apple Tree* by Gail Gibbons

Nonfiction: Things to Make You Think

Read the nonfiction book. Remember that this is a true book and it is important to listen for the facts. Choose from the activities listed below or make up your own.

1. Do apple trees die in the wintertime?

2. What is inside each bud?

3. What happens in the spring that makes the buds open up?

4. What is the first sign that fruit will appear on the tree?

5. What is the job of the sepal?

6. How do insects and birds help change the apple blossom into fruit?

7. Where is the stamen?

8. What is on the very top of the stamen?

9. How is the pistil different from the stamen?

10. Where will the ovary be when the flower turns into an apple?

11. How does the pollen "travel" to another tree to be fertilized so it can become an apple?

12. Why do the petals fall off the tree?

13. Cut an apple open. Ask an adult to help you. Find the "star." Why are the seeds so important?

14. When you go to the grocery store, find the different kinds of apples.

15. Name as many things as you can that involve apples.

Plants and Plant Growth–K

TOPIC: APPLES

NONFICTION: *How Do Apples Grow?* by Betsy Maestro

FICTION: *The Seasons of Arnold's Apple Tree* by Gail Gibbons

Fiction: Things to Make You Think

Read the fiction book. Remember that this book is a made-up story. Choose from the activities listed below or make up your own.

1. Write a story or draw pictures about you and another kind of fruit tree. For example: "Patty's Pear Tree," "Charley's Cherry Tree," "Peter's Plum Tree," "Mary's Mango Tree."

2. Do you have a secret place like Arnold's? Shhh! Don't tell.

3. How does the apple tree keep Arnold busy in the spring?

4. How does the apple tree keep Arnold busy in the summer?

5. How does the apple tree keep Arnold busy in the fall?

6. How does the apple tree keep Arnold busy in the winter?

7. What would the tree say to Arnold if it could talk?

8. If someone wanted to chop down the tree, what would you do or say or write to stop that person?

9. What other fruit trees could keep you busy, as Arnold's apple tree did?

10. What is your favorite fruit? Read about it and find out how it grows.

11. Ask your neighbors about the trees in your neighborhood.

12. What would the Earth be like without trees?

Baby Animals

Animals and Their Needs–K

TOPIC: BABY ANIMALS
NONFICTION: *Baby Animals* by Illa Podendorf
FICTION: *Pig Pig Grows Up* by David McPhail

Nonfiction: Things to Make You Think

Read the nonfiction book. Remember that this is a true book and it is important to listen for the facts. Choose from the activities listed below or make up your own.

1. What does a mother bat do with her baby when she goes out for food?

2. Where do baby opossums live for their first eight weeks of life?

3. What do horses and camels have in common, according to the book?

4. How long does it take a baby rabbit to grow up?

5. Which animal is fully grown in six months?

6. When are most baby bears born? Where are they born?

7. How long does it take a baby elephant to become full grown?

8. Do all baby animals drink milk?

9. How are alligators, turtles, insects, and baby fish alike?

10. What animals change a great deal while growing up?

11. How are all birds alike?

12. How does a mother bird protect her nest?

13. Do snakes sit on their eggs?

14. Do all animals have only one baby at a time?

15. How long does it take a human baby to be born?

Animals and Their Needs–K

TOPIC: BABY ANIMALS
NONFICTION: *Baby Animals* by Illa Podendorf
FICTION: *Pig Pig Grows Up* by David McPhail

Fiction: Things to Make You Think

Read the fiction book. Remember that this book is a made-up story. Choose from the activities listed below or make up your own.

1. What does Pig Pig refuse to do?

2. Do you want to grow up? Why or why not?

3. Does Pig Pig look big enough to walk by himself?

4. Would you push Pig Pig in the stroller?

5. Why is mother tired of Pig Pig's behavior?

6. Why does Pig Pig cry all night long?

7. What clothes does he want to wear?

8. Why does Pig Pig's mother give in to Pig Pig?

9. What happens as Pig Pig's mother tries to push Pig Pig up the hill?

10. What does Pig Pig see that fills his eyes with horror?

11. How does Pig Pig stop the runaway stroller? What would you have done?

12. Why does Pig Pig "beam" when he stops the stroller?

13. How does the runaway stroller ride change Pig Pig?

14. Who is pushed home in the stroller? By whom?

15. Can you still fit into your stroller? Would you want to?

Baby Animals

Directions: Draw a line to match the baby name to the adult name that goes with it.

colt	butterfly
caterpillar	pig
lamb	cat
tadpole	horse
kitten	goose
puppy	lion
fawn	dog
cub	frog
piglet	sheep
gosling	deer

Corn

Plants and Plant Growth–K

TOPIC: CORN

NONFICTION: *Corn Is Maize: The Gift of the Indians* by Aliki

FICTION: *Popcorn* by Frank Asch

Nonfiction: Things to Make You Think

Read the nonfiction book. Remember that this is a true book and it is important to listen for the facts. Choose from the activities listed below or make up your own.

1. A corn seed is hard when planted. How does it get soft enough to sprout?

2. Can you really hear corn grow?

3. What are the female and male parts of corn?

4. Some corn is picked for eating, other ears are left on the stalk. What are the ears that are left used for?

5. Why do corn seeds have to be planted?

6. How are grass plants alike?

7. Where was ancient corn first found?

8. What did Christopher Columbus name the good farmers in the New World?

9. Name some things made from corn.

10. Why did Columbus call corn "maize"?

11. Pilgrims were taught how to plant corn by the Indians. How did the Pilgrims use corn and the corn plant?

12. Try to make a corn husk wreath as shown in the book.

13. If you discovered a new vegetable, what would it be? What would it look like? What would you name it?

14. Make up a new dish using corn.

Plants and Plant Growth–K

TOPIC: CORN
NONFICTION: *Corn Is Maize: The Gift of the Indians* by Aliki
FICTION: *Popcorn* by Frank Asch

Fiction: Things to Make You Think

Read the fiction book. Remember that this book is a made-up story. Choose from the activities listed below or make up your own.

1. At the beginning of the story, what time of year is it?

2. Mama and Papa Bear leave Sam with special directions. What are they?

3. Why does Sam call all his friends?

4. Why does Betty name her popcorn "Blackcat Popcorn"?

5. Why does Billy name his popcorn "Royal Popcorn"?

6. What kind of popcorn does the ghost bring to the party?

7. Do you think Sam is taking good care of the house?

8. Why do they need such a big popcorn pot when they decide to pop the corn?

9. Why does the popcorn fill the kitchen?

10. What happens after the popcorn fills the downstairs?

11. Why does everyone want to go home?

12. How do the bears clean up the house?

13. How do the little bears feel as they leave the party? Have you ever felt that way? When? Why?

14. What is Sam's gift from Mama and Papa?

15. Why isn't Sam smiling on the last page?

CORN

Directions: Number the kernels of popped corn from 1 to 20. Use your best handwriting.

Ears

Human Body–K

TOPIC: EARS

NONFICTION: *You Can't Smell a Flower with Your Ear! All About Your Five Senses* by Joanna Cole

FICTION: *The Ear Book* by Al Perkins

Nonfiction: Things to Make You Think

Read the nonfiction book. Remember that this is a true book and it is important to listen for the facts. Choose from the activities listed below or make up your own.

1. How many sense organs do you have?

2. How does light get into your eyes?

3. Try the experiment in the book. What if your pupils could not get bigger and smaller? How do you think your eyes would feel?

4. Do your eyes work all by themselves? What else do you need?

5. Try the same thing the girl is doing. Did your brain figure it out?

6. What do you see in the black-and-white picture?

7. You can hear vibrations; can you see them?

8. What is the eardrum made of?

9. What connects the ear to the brain?

10. Try the experiment of cupping your hands behind your ears. Did it work?

11. Why can we tell where a sound is coming from?

12. Molecules help you use which of your five senses?

13. Can you see with your nose? Why not?

14. Can you smell with your ear? Why not?

15. Make up a story or poem about the senses getting mixed up.

Human Body–K

TOPIC: EARS

NONFICTION: *You Can't Smell a Flower with Your Ear! All About Your Five Senses* by Joanna Cole

FICTION: *The Ear Book* by Al Perkins

Fiction: Things to Make You Think

Read the fiction book. Remember that this book is a made-up story. Choose from the activities listed below or make up your own.

1. Whose ears will "catch" more sound, the boy's or the dog's?

2. What other sounds can water make besides "drop, drop, drop"? Try making different sounds with water around the house.

3. What are some other things that make the "pop" sound?

4. What do the little lines drawn out from the birds' mouths stand for?

5. What other things might make the sound "toot"?

6. Think of words that rhyme with *ding, dong; ping, pong;* and *sing, song.*

7. Think of some words that rhyme with *snore* and *door.*

8. How is the big drum like the eardrum?

9. Think of some words that rhyme with *clap, snap,* and *tap.*

10. Listen to the sounds in your house. List what you hear.

11. Listen to the sounds outside your house. List what you hear.

12. Draw your own pictures of things that make sounds and use lines to show the vibrations.

13. Can sounds be too loud? Can loud sounds hurt your ears?

14. How can you take good care of your ears?

15. Turn down the TV but watch the screen. Can you figure out what is happening?

EARS

Directions: On the line below each picture write LOUD if the object would have a loud sound and SOFT if the object would have a soft sound.

train

monster truck

traffic light

mouse

fish in a bowl

falling snow

speaker blasting

bugle blaring

drums

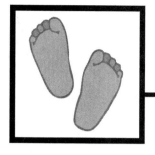

Feet

Human Body–K

TOPIC: FEET

NONFICTION: *My Feet* by Aliki

FICTION: *Alfie's Feet* by Shirley Hughes

Nonfiction: Things to Make You Think

Read the nonfiction book. Remember that this is a true book and it is important to listen for the facts. Choose from the activities listed below or make up your own.

1. What are the three parts of your foot?

2. Why do we have toenails?

3. Try standing on your heels like the kids in the picture.

4. Find the ball of your foot. Is it shaped like any ball you have seen?

5. Wet your foot and then step on a piece of notebook paper, or draw around your foot. Does your arch show? Why or why not?

6. Why do shoe salespeople measure your feet when you go shopping for new shoes?

7. Think up a game like "This Little Piggy" and try it out on a baby.

8. Who has the biggest feet in your family?

9. Why are your feet an important part of your body? List all the things you can do with your feet.

10. Toes are fun. What can you do with your toes?

11. Why is it important to wear shoes most of the time and to be very careful when you go barefoot?

12. Why is it important to wear boots and heavy socks in cold weather?

Human Body–K

TOPIC: FEET

NONFICTION: *My Feet* by Aliki

FICTION: *Alfie's Feet* by Shirley Hughes

Fiction: Things to Make You Think

Read the fiction book. Remember that this book is a made-up story. Choose from the activities listed below or make up your own.

1. What is Alfie's little sister's name?

2. What game is Alfie playing with his little sister?

3. What color are Annie Rose's new shoes?

4. Can Annie Rose walk all by herself?

5. What color are Alfie's shoes?

6. Can Alfie tie his shoes? Can you tie your shoes?

7. Where are Alfie, Annie Rose, and their mother playing?

8. What is Annie Rose doing in the park?

9. How does Alfie warm and dry his feet?

10. Where do Alfie and Mom go one Saturday?

11. What color are Alfie's new boots?

12. Why do you think Alfie is stomping around the house in his boots?

13. Have you ever gone splashing through puddles as Alfie did? Describe how you and your feet felt.

14. Write a short story about your adventure or write a "Puddle Poem."

15. Write about or design boots with the title "These Boots Are Made for Stomping."

16. On the next page, color each boot according to the color written below it.

Red

Blue

Green

Purple

Yellow

Black

Feet II

Human Body–K

TOPIC: FEET II
NONFICTION: *The Foot Book* by Dr. Seuss
FICTION: *Four Fur Feet* by Margaret Wise Brown

Nonfiction: Things to Make You Think

Read the nonfiction book. Remember that this is a true book and it is important to listen for the facts. Choose from the activities listed below or make up your own.

1. Wiggle your left foot.

2. Wiggle your right foot.

3. Touch your left foot with your right hand.

4. Touch your right foot with your left hand.

5. March around the room. Start with your left foot. Say "left, right, left, right" as you march.

6. When do you have slow feet?

7. When do you have fast feet?

8. Have you ever had sick feet? Tell about it.

9. Who has the biggest feet in your family?

10. Who has the smallest feet in your family?

11. Which are your favorite feet in the book?

12. What are the strangest feet you have ever seen?

13. Count the feet you meet when you go for a walk. Remember that some animals have four feet.

14. How many words can you think of that rhyme with "feet"?

Human Body–K

TOPIC: FEET II

NONFICTION: *The Foot Book* by Dr. Seuss

FICTION: *Four Fur Feet* by Margaret Wise Brown

Fiction: Things to Make You Think

Read the fiction book. Remember that this book is a made-up story. Choose from the activities listed below or make up some of your own.

1. What does the yellow furry animal walk on?

2. How many toes does he have?

3. Is he a noisy animal?

4. Can you make a sound like the boat sound?

5. Does the yellow furry animal walk by the river during the day or at night? How do you know?

6. What sound does the train make?

7. What does the yellow furry animal see after the train goes by?

8. What sound do the cows make?

9. How do the four fur feet get wet?

10. How do the four fur feet get dry?

11. How the four fur feet get warm?

12. Name some other places the animals could go on four fur feet.

13. Try to walk on all fours without making any noise.

14. The pictures in this book are very simple yet very interesting. Pick a favorite, and try to draw it like the artist did. Add your own special touches.

FEET II

Directions: Cut out the pictures of the feet. Use them as a pattern and make as many as you need to play GO FOOT, which is played just like GO FISH. You can also use the feet to leave a trail for someone to follow.

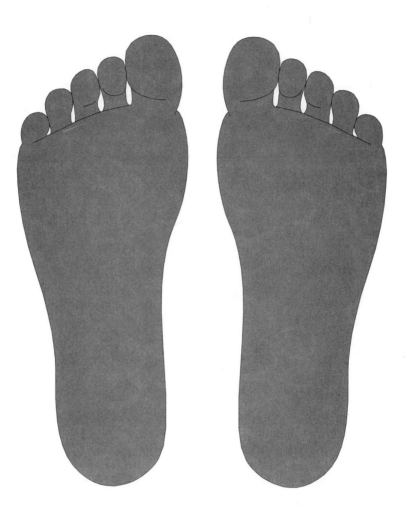

Hands

Human Body–K

TOPIC: HANDS

NONFICTION: *My Hands* by Aliki

FICTION: *Hanimations* by Mario Mariotti

Nonfiction: Things to Make You Think

Read the nonfiction book. Remember that this is a true book and it is important to listen for the facts. Choose from the activities listed below or make up your own.

1. What finger games have you played?

2. Raise your right hand and wiggle your fingers.

3. Raise your left hand and wiggle your fingers.

4. Name your fingers on each hand.

5. How do fingernails help the hands and help us?

6. Which finger is very different from the other four? How?

7. Try to hold a pencil without using your thumb. Can you draw or write?

8. What is the largest part of your hand called?

9. What can you do with the palms of your hands?

10. Are you ambidextrous? Do you know anyone who is?

11. Are everyone's hands exactly the same? Why or why not?

12. Compare your family's hands. How are they alike and how are they different?

13. Count all the ways you use your hands during the next hour.

14. How can you take care of your hands so they can take care of you?

15. Close your eyes and touch different things around the house. Have an adult guide you around. How do your fingers and hands help you?

Human Body–K

TOPIC: HANDS

NONFICTION: *My Hands* by Aliki

FICTION: *Hanimations* by Mario Mariotti

Fiction: Things to Make You Think

Read the fiction book. Remember that this book is a made-up story. Choose from the activities listed below or make up your own.

1. Which hand is the "crab" in the first picture?

2. How many hands are in the second picture?

3. Find the picture of the peacock. How many fingers do you see? How many thumbs?

4. What fingers make the ears of the black-and-white dog?

5. How many hands does it take to make the alligator? Which finger is the tongue?

6. What is used to make the spines on the porcupine?

7. Find the picture of the horse. What color is the horse's mane?

8. Find the fangs on the yellow snake. What color are they?

9. What do you see on the page with the X rays of the hands? Why do they look so scared?

10. How many people are needed to make the orange animal with the black spots?

11. Pick a hanimation that you like and write or tell a story about it.

12. Try to make the same shapes with your hands. Do not paint your own hands unless you ask an adult to help.

13. Shadow puppets are also fun to do. Shine a flashlight on the wall and use your hands to make different shapes on the wall. What did you make?

14. Trace your own hand and color a design on it just for fun.

HANDS

Directions: Draw a line from the word to the correct part of the hand.

palm

thumb

index finger

middle finger

ring finger

little finger (pinkie)

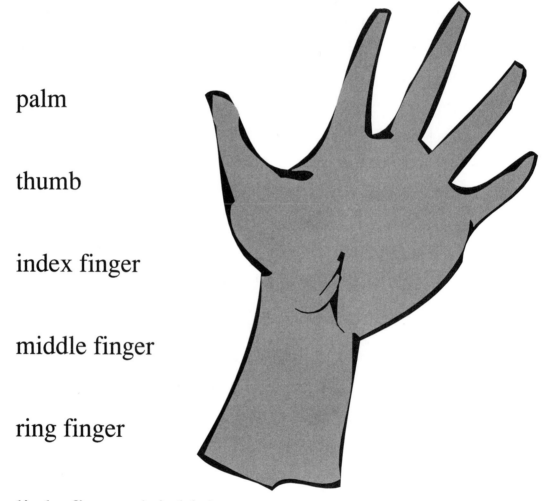

Pigs

Farm–K

TOPIC: PIGS

NONFICTION: *Pigs Will Be Pigs* by Amy Axelrod

FICTION: *The Three Little Pigs* by James Marshall

Nonfiction: Things to Make You Think

Read the nonfiction book. Remember that this is a true book and it is important to listen for the facts. Choose from the activities listed below or make up your own.

1. What do you think made the pigs think about food?

2. Check out the fridge! What are some of the foods the pigs have already eaten?

3. What are some other ways to pay if you do not have cash money?

4. What pets do the pigs have?

5. Have you ever had a "hunt for money" at your house? What did you find?

6. Have you ever seen a $2 bill? Whose picture is on it?

7. How much does Mrs. Pig find in the bedroom?

8. How much is 200 pennies?

9. How much do the children find in all?

10. How much do the pigs find in the front hall closet?

11. How do you suppose the $5 bill got wet?

12. Where do the pigs go to dinner? What kind of restaurant is it?

13. Have your family decide what they would like for dinner. Figure out how much the whole dinner would cost.

14. Do you think it was worth messing up the house so badly for the amount of money the pigs found?

15. Check your math against the answers on the last page. How did you do?

Farm–K

TOPIC: PIGS

NONFICTION: *Pigs Will Be Pigs* by Amy Axelrod

FICTION: *The Three Little Pigs* by James Marshall

Fiction: Things to Make You Think

Read the fiction book. Remember that this book is a made-up story. Choose from the activities listed below or make up your own.

1. What is a sow?

2. Why do you think the man says, "That's not a good idea" to the first little pig?

3. Is the first little pig rude to the man, in your opinion? What could he have said that would have been more polite?

4. How does the wolf get to the first little pig's house?

5. Do you think it would be hard to blow over a straw house?

6. What is the second little pig's house made of?

7. Why do you think the stick house is built on stilts?

8. What are the two decorations hanging at the corner of the stick house called?

9. The wolf eats two little pigs. Do you think he is greedy to go after the third?

10. Do you think the third little pig is smart? Why or why not?

11. Why does the third little pig always make plans to meet the wolf later?

12. Why is the wolf getting "put out"? What does that mean?

13. Does the wolf try to beat the pig at his own game? How?

14. The wolf thinks he is being nice. What do you think?

15. Draw a picture of a house you might want to build.

PIGS

Directions: Cut out the pigs and put them in number order.

Puddles

Seasons and Weather–K

TOPIC: PUDDLES
NONFICTION: *Where Do Puddles Go?* by Fay Robinson
FICTION: *The Puddle* by David McPhail

Nonfiction: Things to Make You Think

Read the nonfiction book. Remember that this is a true book and it is important to listen for the facts. Choose from the activities listed below or make up your own.

1. What is the title of the book?

2. What do you think the child on the cover is looking at?

3. Do you like to watch the rain?

4. Have you ever jumped in puddles? Did you have boots on? What happened?

5. Have you ever watched a puddle disappear?

6. What helps puddles disappear?

7. Where do the little drops of water go?

8. Can you see water vapor?

9. Explain "evaporation" in your own words.

10. Explain "condensation" in your own words.

11. Why are some clouds darker than others?

12. What are clouds made of?

13. Why does it snow sometimes instead of rain?

14. Draw your own picture to show the water cycle.

15. Why is it so important not to waste water?

Seasons and Weather–K

TOPIC: PUDDLES

NONFICTION: *Where Do Puddles Go?* by Fay Robinson

FICTION: *The Puddle* by David McPhail

Fiction: Things to Make You Think

Read the fiction book. Remember that this book is a made-up story. Choose from the activities listed below or make up some of your own.

1. What is the boy doing on the first page of the story?

2. What is he going to do in the puddles?

3. How is he going to stay dry?

4. Does the frog like the boat?

5. Do you think the boy is upset with the frog?

6. How is the turtle floating?

7. Why can't the boy have tea with the turtle?

8. What happens to the frog and the turtle?

9. Who offers to help the boy get his boat back?

10. What happens to the boat?

11. Do you think the puddle is big enough for a pig to swim in?

12. Why is the boy upset with the pig?

13. Why are all the animals upset with the elephant?

14. Could this story really have happened?

15. What makes this story more interesting than just a boy playing in a puddle?

16. What do you think the artist used to paint the pictures for this book?

PUDDLES

Directions: Put the following words from the books in alphabetical order.

sun   cloud   rain drops   waterfall   puddle

boat   turtle   elephant   alligator   boots

1. _____

2. _____

3. _____

4. _____

5. _____

6. _____

7. _____

8. _____

9. _____

10. _____

Seeds

Plants and Plant Growth–K

TOPIC: SEEDS
NONFICTION: *How a Seed Grows* by Helene J. Jordan
FICTION: *The Carrot Seed* by Ruth Krauss

Nonfiction: Things to Make You Think

Read the nonfiction book. Remember that this is a true book and it is important to listen for the facts. Choose from the activities listed below or make up your own.

1. Do all seeds grow at the same speed?

2. What tree seed grows very slowly?

3. What seed grows into a plant in just a few weeks?

4. Plant your own bean seeds as shown in the book.

5. What does the seed look like on day three?

6. What does the seed look like on day five?

7. What will happen next?

8. Where do the root hairs grow?

9. First the roots push down, but then they push toward what energy source?

10. After the shoots push up, what happens?

11. What three things does a seed need to grow?

12. Will an apple tree grow into an oak tree? How do you know?

13. Look at trees when you are outside. How are they different?

14. Name some things that are the same about trees.

15. Write a story about a tree that lives in your yard.

Plants and Plant Growth–K

TOPIC: SEEDS
NONFICTION: *How a Seed Grows* by Helene J. Jordan
FICTION: *The Carrot Seed* by Ruth Krauss

Fiction: Things to Make You Think

Read the fiction book. Remember that this book is a made-up story. Choose from the activities listed below or make up your own.

1. Have you ever been very sure of something and no one would believe you, like the little boy in the story? Tell about it.

2. Does the little boy give up on the seed even though everyone tells him, "I'm afraid it won't come up"?

3. How do you know he believes in what he is doing?

4. How do you think the little boy feels when the carrot starts to grow?

5. Why does the little boy pull the weeds every day?

6. Why does he water the seed every day?

7. Are the members of his family being mean to him? Why or why not?

8. Tell or write about a time when you had to wait a long, long time for something to happen. Was it easy or hard for you to wait?

9. Tell or write about a time when you planted something. What happened?

10. How do you think the little boy's family feels when he picks the carrot?

11. How do you think the little boy feels when he picks the carrot?

12. Write a story about the "giant carrot."

SEEDS

Directions: Draw a picture of each of the four growth stages of a plant.

seed

sprout

bud

fully grown plant

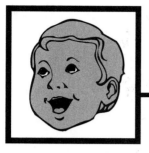

Skin

Human Body, Five Senses, Touch–K

TOPIC: SKIN

NONFICTION: *Your Skin and Mine* by Paul Showers

FICTION: *No Bath Tonight* by Jane Yolen

Nonfiction: Things to Make You Think

Read the nonfiction book. Remember that this is a true book and it is important to listen for the facts. Choose from the activities listed below or make up your own.

1. Find a magnifying glass and look at your skin carefully. What do you see?

2. What is another word for "follicle"?

3. What is in the follicle that keeps your hair soft and shiny?

4. Look at your fingerprint. Use a stamp pad to make your own fingerprints. You can make pictures with your fingerprints. Try it.

5. Fingerprints are like snowflakes. Explain.

6. What is the purpose of fingernails and toenails?

7. Why doesn't it hurt when you cut your hair and nails?

8. What are pores? Are they the same as follicles?

9. What are the names of the two layers of skin?

10. How is a scab like a bandage?

11. Skin is very important. Why do we need it?

12. What protects our skin from burning rays of the sun?

13. What is in the skin that makes it darker?

14. What are freckles really?

15. Why is skin easier to wash than clothes?

Human Body, Five Senses, Touch–K

TOPIC: SKIN
NONFICTION: *Your Skin and Mine* by Paul Showers
FICTION: *No Bath Tonight* by Jane Yolen

Fiction: Things to Make You Think

Read the fiction book. Remember that this book is a made-up story. Choose from the activities listed below or make up your own.

1. Jeremy hurts his foot. Would a bath hurt his foot more?

2. How many berries does Jeremy find?

3. Why doesn't he want to take a bath after picking berries?

4. When you slide into base you should slide in feet first. Why?

5. Do you think you could slide into base and not get dirty?

6. Do you ever paint yourself with paint or markers? Does it stain your skin? Will it ever come off?

7. Why does Jeremy have bandages on?

8. Why is cutting grass a dirty job?

9. Does grass stain your skin? Does it stain your clothes?

10. Jeremy cuts his epidermis and what else?

11. How long has it been since Jeremy has had a bath?

12. What does Grandma mean by "kid leaves"?

13. How does Grandma know about the sand, the paint, and the berries?

14. The dog has been very helpful. What has he done to help?

15. Why doesn't Jeremy need a bath tonight?

Sleep

Human Body–K

TOPIC: SLEEP
NONFICTION: *Sleep Is for Everyone* by Paul Showers
FICTION: *Where the Wild Things Are* by Maurice Sendak

Nonfiction: Things to Make You Think

Read the nonfiction book. Remember that this is a true book and it is important to listen for the facts. Choose from the activities listed below or make up your own.

1. Can snakes close their eyes? Why or why not?

2. What animal can sleep standing up?

3. Why do you think babies need so much sleep?

4. What are you like when you do not get enough sleep?

5. Can anyone get along without sleep?

6. When does your body need rest?

7. Does your brain rest when you are awake?

8. What keeps your heart and lungs working while you are asleep?

9. What does the experiment in the book prove?

10. Is it a good idea to try and stay up when you are tired?

11. What do you dream about? Describe a dream you have had.

12. The pictures in this book could be made by tearing or cutting construction or any colored paper into shapes. Try making your own dream picture.

Human Body–K

TOPIC: SLEEP

NONFICTION: *Sleep Is for Everyone* by Paul Showers

FICTION: *Where the Wild Things Are* by Maurice Sendak

Fiction: Things to Make You Think

Read the fiction book. Remember that this book is a made-up story. Choose from the activities listed below or make up your own.

1. Who wrote this story and made the illustrations?

2. Why is Max sent to bed without his dinner?

3. How does Max's room grow a forest?

4. What is the name of the boat?

5. Where is Max sailing?

6. What does Max find after "sailing" for a while?

7. Is Max afraid of the wild things?

8. How does Max tame all the wild things?

9. What do the "king" and all the wild things do during the "rumpus"?

10. Why do the wild things want Max to stay?

11. What is waiting for Max when he "sails" back through time?

12. Has Max been gone very long?

13. What is Max really doing?

14. Draw a picture of your own "wild thing" that might live in the forest.

15. Tell or write about Max and the wild things during another dream. What adventures might they have?

SLEEP

Directions: Draw a picture of yourself when you are awake and when you are asleep.

Sleep

Awake

Touch

Human Body–K

TOPIC: TOUCH

NONFICTION: *I Can Tell by Touching* by Carolyn Otto

FICTION: *Great Thumbprint Drawing Book* by Ed Emberley

Nonfiction: Things to Make You Think

Read the nonfiction book. Remember that this is a true book and it is important to listen for the facts. Choose from the activities listed below or make up your own.

1. The sense of touch is one of our five senses. What are the other four?

2. What does your chair feel like?

3. What else would feel waxy like a crayon?

4. Describe what you can feel right now.

5. Describe the difference between the feel of a potato and that of an egg.

6. Feel the page of the book. How does it feel?

7. Would a bunny's fur feel the same as your hair?

8. In each of three small bowls or small plastic bags put 1 teaspoon of sugar, salt, and flour. See if you can label each correctly by touching. Have someone help you with this experiment.

9. Touch the head of three stuffed animals or dolls. Can you tell which is which?

10. Walk barefoot on carpet and then on a hard floor. Tell how they feel.

11. Close your eyes and feel your way around your room. Be careful and wear shoes. Tell what you are touching as you move around your room.

12. Collect leaves from trees and plants. Do they all feel the same? Describe how they feel.

Human Body–K

TOPIC: TOUCH
NONFICTION: *I Can Tell by Touching* by Carolyn Otto
FICTION: *Great Thumbprint Drawing Book* by Ed Emberley

Fiction: Things to Make You Think

Read the fiction book. Remember that this book is a made-up story. Choose from the activities listed below or make up some of your own.

1. Who is the author of this drawing book?

2. Can you name all the thumbprint pictures on the cover?

3. What words does the book use to help draw the pictures?

4. How are the directions like a math problem?

5. Are the letters always going to look like letters?

6. Are all thumbprints the same?

7. How could you make different-sized characters?

8. What is a critter?

9. What is the section titled "Folks" showing you?

10. What does the section titled "Action" show you how to do?

11. Could you also use your fingerprints to make pictures?

12. What other prints might be interesting?

TOUCH

Directions: Much of the touching we do is with our fingertips. Use an inkpad and make as many thumbprint and fingerprint drawings as you want or have time to do.

Weather

Seasons and Weather–K

TOPIC: WEATHER
NONFICTION: *What Will the Weather Be?* by Lynda DeWitt
FICTION: *Cloudy with a Chance of Meatballs* by Judi Barrett

Nonfiction: Things to Make You Think

Read the nonfiction book. Remember that this is a true book and it is important to listen for the facts. Choose from the following activities or make up some of your own.

1. What does it mean to predict the weather?

2. What is the line between the new air and the old air called?

3. What does a thermometer measure?

4. What does an anemometer measure?

5. What does a hygrometer measure?

6. What does a barometer measure?

7. Explain aloud or on paper the water cycle during a cold front

8. Explain aloud or on paper the water cycle during a warm front.

9. Tell which front you would like to have forming if you were planning the following activities:

   a. a ski trip

   b. an all-day sailing trip

   c. planting a garden

   d. hoping for a day off from school

   e. an all-day soccer tournament

10. What is the job of a meteorologist?

11. Name five different places where weather instruments can be found.

12. Find the weather map in the newspaper or on television. Can you find some of the symbols from the book and tell what they mean?

13. Are the forecasts always correct? Why or why not?

Seasons and Weather–K

TOPIC: WEATHER
NONFICTION: *What Will the Weather Be?* by Lynda DeWitt
FICTION: *Cloudy with a Chance of Meatballs* by Judi Barrett

Fiction: Things to Make You Think

Read the fiction book. Remember that this is a made-up story. Choose from the activities listed below or make up some of your own.

1. Where is the town of Chewandswallow?

2. Why aren't there any food stores in Chewandswallow?

3. Write or tell about a forecast for a day in the town of Chewandswallow.

4. How do the townspeople prepare for all kinds of weather?

5. What happens that closes the school?

6. What kind of tornado hit?

7. Why do the people leave Chewandswallow?

8. What do the townspeople build their homes out of when they reach their new town?

9. Grandpa is a super tall tale storyteller. Using exaggeration, make up a tall tale about something you do on a daily or weekly basis, such as taking out the garbage or piano lessons.

10. Explain how you would clean up the spaghetti mess in Chewandswallow. Invent a new machine.

11. Make up your own story. Here are some story starters:

     Sunny with a chance of . . .

     High winds likely bringing in . . .

12. List five of your favorite foods. Give a weather forecast using those foods. Name the four weather instruments you would use to make your forecast.

WEATHER

Directions: Draw a line from the weather instrument to the condition it measures.

thermometer   air speed

hygrometer   air pressure

barometer   wind direction

wind vane   temperature

anemometer   humidity

Wind

Seasons and Weather–K

TOPIC: WIND

NONFICTION: *Feel the Wind* by Arthur Dorros

FICTION: *Millicent and the Wind* by Robert Munsch

Nonfiction: Things to Make You Think

Read the nonfiction book. Remember that this is a true book and it is important to listen for the facts. Choose from the activities listed below or make up your own.

1. What is wind?

2. What pushes clouds across the sky?

3. Can you make air move? How? Try different ways.

4. Explain how wind is made.

5. Where on Earth is the air the hottest?

6. Where on Earth is the air the coldest?

7. Why does hot air rise?

8. What rushes in to take the place of rising hot air? Why?

9. Which would get hotter on a summer day, the sidewalk or the grass?

10. Which gets hotter faster, air over land or air over water?

11. Wind helps us in many ways. Name some.

12. Wind can be harmful. How?

13. Why do winds have names?

14. Can you ever see heat waves? When might this happen?

Seasons and Weather–K

TOPIC: WIND
NONFICTION: *Feel the Wind* by Arthur Dorros
FICTION: *Millicent and the Wind* by Robert Munsch

Fiction: Things to Make You Think

Read the fiction book. Remember that this book is a made-up story. Choose from the activities listed below or make up your own.

1. Why doesn't Millicent have any friends?

2. Who is talking to Millicent?

3. Have you ever heard the wind "talk"?

4. The wind and Millicent have fun together. What would you play if the wind were your friend?

5. Why can't the wind find Millicent when she goes into the valley?

6. How long does it take Mom and Millicent to reach the valley where other people live?

7. Why do you think the children are mean to Millicent?

8. Why does the wind toss the boy into the air?

9. Why is Millicent sad that the children ran away?

10. Have you ever felt lonely? What did you do about it?

11. Where do you think the boy came from?

12. How do you know this is a made-up story?

13. If you were the wind and could go anywhere in the world, where would you go?

14. Find the weather map in the newspaper. Can you tell which way the wind is blowing?

WIND

Directions: Label the following pictures using the word list.

windsock   windmill   tornado   weather vane
windsurfing   windy   old man winter

_____   _____   _____

_____   _____   _____

_____

Grade

1

Air

Matter–1

TOPIC: AIR

NONFICTION: *Air Is All Around You* by Franklyn M. Branley

FICTION: *The Big Balloon Race* by Eleanor Coerr

Nonfiction: Things to Make You Think

Read the nonfiction book. Remember that this is a true book and it is important to listen for the facts. Choose from the activities listed below or make up your own.

1. Where is air?

2. Can you see air?

3. How can you feel air?

4. Read the experiment in the book with the glass and paper napkin. Try it. What did you learn?

5. What keeps the napkin dry?

6. How does the food coloring in the water help you see what is happening in the glass?

7. How is an orange peel like the air around the Earth?

8. How much does the air weigh?

9. Can you count to 5 quadrillion by millions? Start with 500 million and keep adding three zeros and you will have 500 billion then 500 trillion then 500 quadrillion.

10. Spaceships cannot fly in outer space. They need to be rocketed into outer space and then travel in an _____.

11. Is there air in outer space? How do you know?

12. Is there air in the ocean? How do you know?

13. Name two places where human beings need to take air with them and explain why.

14. Try the experiment with the two glasses of water.

Matter–1

TOPIC: AIR

NONFICTION: *Air Is All Around You* by Franklyn M. Branley

FICTION: *The Big Balloon Race* by Eleanor Coerr

Fiction: Things to Make You Think

Read the fiction book. Remember that this book is a made-up story. Choose from the activities listed below or make up some of your own.

1. What does Ariel want to do?

2. What is Ariel's mother's name?

3. On what kind of farm do Ariel and her parents live?

4. What is an aeronaut?

5. What kind of gas fills the balloons that are going to race?

6. Who is the greatest gentleman aeronaut, according to the story?

7. Who is the greatest lady aeronaut, according to the story?

8. Why does Ariel fall asleep in the basket?

9. Why is Ariel a problem for Carlotta in the balloon basket?

10. What is an updraft?

11. Why does the balloon finally come down out of the rain cloud?

12. How would an air stream help Carlotta and Ariel win the race?

13. What happens when they go lower to catch the air stream?

14. What do they have to do to make the basket lighter to make it over the lake?

15. How does Ariel help win the race in the end?

AIR

Directions: Label the parts of the hot air balloon using the word list. Then design and color your own hot air balloon.

Word List:

balloon   sand bag   basket   heat   hydrogen gas

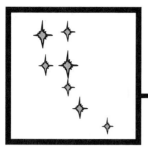

Big Dipper

Astronomy, Constellations–1

TOPIC: BIG DIPPER
NONFICTION: *The Big Dipper* by Franklyn M. Branley
FICTION: *Follow the Drinking Gourd* by Jeanette Winter

Nonfiction: Things to Make You Think

Read the nonfiction book. Remember that this is a true book and the facts are important. Choose from the activities listed below or make up your own.

1. Why are the stars bright only on some nights?

2. Are the stars always in the same place in the sky all year?

3. What stars can you see during both summer and winter?

4. How did the Big Dipper get its name?

5. How many stars are in the Big Dipper?

6. Can you name the stars in the Big Dipper?

7. Why are the Big Dipper and the North Star so important to travelers?

8. What is another name for the North Star?

9. What star is the end of the handle of the Little Dipper?

10. What does "Ursa Major" mean?

11. Why do you need to use your imagination when star gazing?

12. What does "Ursa Minor" mean?

13. Why do the kids have a compass while trying to find the Big Dipper?

14. Why is it easier to imagine shapes while gazing at the clouds?

15. Do you know names of other constellations?

16. Try to find the Big Dipper and the Little Dipper some night soon.

Astronomy, Constellations–1

TOPIC: BIG DIPPER
NONFICTION: *The Big Dipper* by Franklyn M. Branley
FICTION: *Follow the Drinking Gourd* by Jeanette Winter

Fiction: Things to Make You Think

Read the fiction book. Remember that this is a made-up story even though it is based on real happenings. Choose from the activities listed below or make up your own.

1. Who is Peg Leg Joe?

2. Why do you think he wants to help the slaves?

3. Why do you think the Big Dipper is called a drinking gourd?

4. What is a gourd? Use a dictionary to find out if you don't know.

5. How are families split up? Why?

6. Why do Molly and James decide to follow the drinking gourd?

7. Why does the family travel at night and hide in the trees during the day?

8. How does singing the song help the runaway slave family?

9. What happens if it is cloudy and they can't see the stars?

10. What are the dangers they have to face to follow the drinking gourd?

11. Who helps the family along the way?

12. How do you think the family feels when they finally spot Peg Leg Joe?

13. Where does Joe take the family?

14. Why was freedom so important to the slaves? Imagine what it would be like if you could never leave your house or yard. What are some of the things you would miss?

15. Explain the meaning of "Underground Railroad." Harriet Tubman also helped people along their way to freedom on the Underground Railroad. You can find out more information and many other wonderful stories at the library.

BIG DIPPER

Directions: Draw the positions of the Big Dipper for each season of the year. North should be the top of your paper.

Summer

Fall

Winter

Spring

Camouflage

Living Things and Their Environments–1

TOPIC: CAMOUFLAGE
NONFICTION: *What Color Is Camouflage?* by Carolyn Otto
FICTION: *Elmer* by David McKee

Nonfiction: Things to Make You Think

Read the nonfiction book. Remember that this is a true book and it is important to listen for the facts. Choose from the activities listed below or make up your own.

1. Why is the mountain lion hard to see in the picture?

2. Why would the dog not want to chase a skunk?

3. How many different animals can you find in the picture?

4. Why is the baby deer spotted?

5. Why must the baby deer or fawn stay very quiet at times?

6. "Disguise" is another word for "camouflage." Have you ever worn a disguise? Write or tell about it.

7. How many chipmunks can you find in the picture?

8. Why is a red fox red?

9. Why do some animals change color for different seasons of the year?

10. Name some animals that change color very quickly to hide.

11. Name some animals that protect themselves by being easy to see.

12. Can you find the hidden animals in the picture in the book?

13. How would people camouflage themselves?

14. Why would people want to camouflage themselves?

Living Things and Their Environments–1

TOPIC: CAMOUFLAGE

NONFICTION: *What Color Is Camouflage?* by Carolyn Otto

FICTION: *Elmer* by David McKee

Fiction: Things to Make You Think

Read the fiction book. Remember that this book is a made-up story. Choose from the activities listed below or make up your own.

1. Elmer is a member of a _____ of elephants.

2. Are all the elephants exactly alike?

3. How many different colors are on Elmer's skin?

4. Elmer keeps all the other elephants happy. Do you know a person like Elmer?

5. Does Elmer like being laughed at?

6. Why does he leave one morning?

7. Elmer is looking for elephant-colored berries. What does he do when he finds them?

8. Elmer tries to camouflage his patchwork skin with berries. Think of some other ways to help Elmer.

9. Why isn't Elmer happy? How does he feel? Have you ever felt like Elmer? Tell or write about it.

10.   How many animals can you find in the picture? Can you name them all?

11. Can you find Elmer in the picture?

12. What happens every year now to celebrate "Elmer's Best Joke"?

13. Draw a picture of how you would disguise yourself on Elmer's Parade Day.

14. Elmer is like the "class clown." Is there someone you know who is fun like Elmer? Tell or write about that person. You may want to write to that person telling how much you appreciate his or her humor.

CAMOUFLAGE

Directions: Write each animal's name under the word that tells how it is camouflaged

Word List:

jackrabbit   fawn   red bat   hermit crab
walking stick   fox   bobcat
common   octopus
   whippoorwill

COLOR   **PATTERN**   **SHAPE**

_____   _____   _____

_____   _____   _____

_____   _____   _____

_____   _____   _____

_____   _____   _____

_____   _____   _____

_____   _____   _____

City Habitats

Living Things and Their Environments–1

TOPIC: CITY HABITATS
NONFICTION: *Falcons Nest on Skyscrapers* by Priscilla Belz Jenkins
FICTION: *Make Way for Ducklings* by Robert McCloskey

Nonfiction: Things to Make You Think

Read the nonfiction book. Remember that this is a true book and it is important to listen for the facts. Choose from the activities listed below or make up your own.

1. Why have falcons been admired for thousands of years?

2. How many kinds of falcons live in the United States?

3. Why are falcons called "birds of prey"?

4. Prove that the falcon is a very fast bird.

5. How do ornithologists study the disappearing falcons?

6. Why are the falcons disappearing?

7. How do researchers go about saving the peregrine falcon?

8. Why do the researchers tag the baby falcons?

9. Where does Scarlett land?

10. What is a "scrape"?

11. How many years does it take for Scarlett to find a mate?

12. How long will falcon mates stay together?

13. Tell why this is a success story for:

    a. Scarlett and Beauregard

    b. The Hawk Barn Scientists

    c. The world

14. Look up more about falcons at your library. There is more to learn!

Living Things and Their Environments–1

TOPIC: CITY HABITATS

NONFICTION: *Falcons Nest on Skyscrapers* by Priscilla Belz Jenkins

FICTION: *Make Way for Ducklings* by Robert McCloskey

Fiction: Things to Make You Think

Read the fiction book. Remember that this book is a made-up story. Choose from the activities listed below or make up your own.

1. Why does Mrs. Mallard decide the pond is a good place to raise ducklings? Why are these reasons important?

2. Why do the Mallards follow the boat?

3. Is the island a better place to nest? Why or why not?

4. What are the "horrid things" Mrs. Mallard is upset about?

5. Mr. and Mrs. Mallard make it to the island just in time. What does this mean?

6. What river do they fly over?

7. Where does the family finally build a nest?

8. What is the policeman's name?

9. Can you name the eight ducklings?

10. Is Mrs. Mallard a good mother? How do you know?

11. Where are Mrs. Mallard and all the ducklings going when they leave the river?

12. What does it mean to have "all your ducks in a row"?

13. Who helps the Mallards cross the busy street?

14. Why does Michael hurry back to the police booth?

15. What kind of store is at the corner?

16. How do the ducks say "thank you"?

17. Who is waiting for them in the Public Gardens?

CITY HABITATS

Directions: Which words below go with the duck and which ones go with the falcon?
Write them on the lines below the picture of each bird.

quack   fished   fastest   merlin   eyries
scrape   stoop   friendly   waddled   swim

FALCON   **DUCK**

_____   _____

_____   _____

_____   _____

_____   _____

_____   _____

_____   _____

Deserts

Living Things and Their Environments–1

TOPIC: DESERTS

NONFICTION: *Desert* by Chris Arvetis

FICTION: *Way Out West Lives a Coyote Named Frank* by J. Lund

Nonfiction: Things to Make You Think

Read the nonfiction book. Remember that this is a true book and it is important to listen for the facts. Choose from the activities listed below or make up your own.

1. Why is Owl carrying a canteen around his neck with H_2O printed on it? What do you think is in the canteen?

2. What is the largest desert in the world?

3. What animal lives in an "ice desert"?

4. How are sand dunes made?

5. Draw a picture showing the difference between a mesa and a butte.

6. Is it hot at night in the desert?

7. Does it rain in the desert every year?

8. What is a "playa"?

9. Why does the turtle say, "Enjoy this while you can"?

10. Where can Owl refill his canteen?

11. Why can a cactus live in the desert where there is so little water for plants?

12. Are there any flowers in the desert? Can you draw and name some?

13. Why do desert animals burrow underground?

14. Choose your favorite animals of the desert. Why do you like them?

15. Frog learns more about the desert after visiting. Did you learn anything new? Tell about what you learned.

Living Things and Their Environments–1

TOPIC: DESERTS

NONFICTION: *Desert* by Chris Arvetis

FICTION: *Way Out West Lives a Coyote Named Frank* by J. Lund

Fiction: Things to Make You Think

Read the fiction book. Remember that this book is a made-up story. Choose from the activities listed below or make up your own.

1. What is the place where Frank lives called?

2. What are the plants near Frank in the picture at the beginning of the book called?

3. What do Frank and Larry do for fun?

4. Why don't Frank and Larry chase porcupines and skunks anymore?

5. Why do Frank and Melanie get along so well?

6. Look at the picture. What do they both like to do? Can you do that?

7. Scorpions and rattlesnakes live in the desert. Why do Frank and Melanie stay away from them?

8. What does Frank do when he is alone?

9. What do you do when you are alone?

10. What new interest does Frank find?

11. Why do you think coyotes howl at the moon?

12. Have you ever seen a desert? What do you remember about it?

13. Why do you think Frank has sunglasses on and a scarf around his neck?

14. What are the shapes of the mountains on the cover of the book called?

15. Would you like to have Frank for a friend? Why or why not?

Dinosaur Extinction

Living Things and Their Environments–1

TOPIC: DINOSAUR EXTINCTION

NONFICTION: *What Happened to the Dinosaurs?* by Franklyn M. Branley

FICTON: *What Happened to Patrick's Dinosaurs?* by C. Carrick

Nonfiction: Things to Make You Think

Read the nonfiction book. Remember that this is a true book and it is important to listen for the facts. Choose from the activities listed below or make up your own.

1. How long did dinosaurs live on Earth?

2. What is a theory?

3. Why do you think theories are important?

4. Why do scientists need theories?

5. Did all dinosaurs lay eggs?

6. Could sickness have wiped out the dinosaurs?

7. Do you think the sun cooled off for a period of time? Why or why not?

8. What do you think of the "shower of meteorites" theory?

9. Why is the twin sun called "Nemesis"?

10. Do we have to worry about a major comet collision in our lifetimes?

11. When is the next one predicted?

12. There are many theories about why the dinosaurs disappeared. Which one do you think is best?

13. Do you have a theory or idea of your own?

Living Things and Their Environments–1

TOPIC: DINOSAUR EXTINCTION
NONFICTION: *What Happened to the Dinosaurs?* by Franklyn M. Branley
FICTON: *What Happened to Patrick's Dinosaurs?* by C. Carrick

Fiction: Things to Make You Think

Read the fiction book. Remember that this book is a made-up story. Choose from the activities listed below or make up your own.

1. Patrick has his own idea or theory about how the dinosaurs lived. In what ways could the dinosaurs help people if we were all here together?

2. In Patrick's imagination, who builds the houses when people and dinosaurs live together?

3. Do you think Hank shares his banana with Patrick?

4. In Patrick's dinosaur world, who is smarter, the people or the dinosaurs?

5. What kind of a dinosaur makes a great bridge for the cars?

6. Do you think Patrick likes raking leaves?

7. The dinosaur circus looks like fun. If you were a dinosaur, what would you do in the circus?

8. Why do the dinosaurs in Patrick's dinosaur world leave Earth?

9. What do the boys see moving across the night sky?

10. Draw a picture of your neighborhood with dinosaurs in it.

11. Use your imagination and tell or write a story about a dinosaur at Disney World.

12. The pictures in this book are wonderful. Pick your favorite and tell why you like it the best.

DINOSAUR EXTINCTION

Directions: Cut out the picture of the bone and use it as a pattern. Trace around the bone to make more. Write the following words from the books on the bones. Put them in alphabetical order or use them as flash cards to study spelling.

egg	meteorites	comet	theory
bones	soot	iridium	carbon
fossils	reptiles	diseases	mystery
	Nemesis	dinosaur	

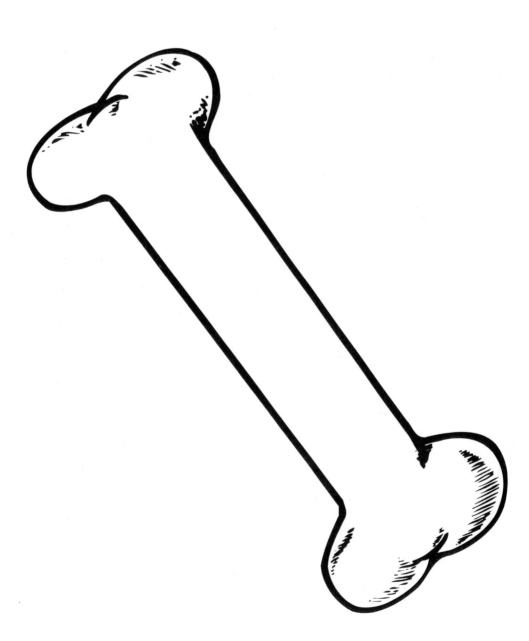

Dinosaurs

Living Things and Their Environments-1

TOPIC: DINOSAURS

NONFICTION: *My Visit to the Dinosaurs* by Aliki

FICTION: *The Dinosaur Who Lived in My Backyard* by B. G. Hennessy

Nonfiction: Things to Make You Think

Read the nonfiction book. Remember that this is a true book and it is important to listen for the facts. Choose from the activities listed or make up your own.

1. Where do the kids go to see dinosaurs?

2. Why do you think some of the bones had to be made of plaster?

3. Why does the skeleton in the museum have to be held together by wire and rods?

4. What year was the first dinosaur fossil found?

5. What is a paleontologist? Would you like to do what paleontologists do?

6. Name three carnivorous dinosaurs.

7. Name three herbivorous dinosaurs.

8. Plan a meal for a carnivore and an herbivore coming to dinner at your house.

9. Why could some dinosaurs live in swamps without drowning?

10. Which dinosaur was the longest?

11. Which dinosaur reminds you of a duck?

12. Which dinosaur was fast enough to catch birds?

13. Which dinosaur had no teeth?

14. Do you think dinosaurs were smart? Why or why not?

15. Why is Tyrannosaurus called the "King of the Dinosaurs"?

Living Things and Their Environments–1

TOPIC: DINOSAURS
NONFICTION: *My Visit to the Dinosaurs* by Aliki
FICTION: *The Dinosaur Who Lived in My Backyard* by B. G. Hennessy

Fiction: Things to Make You Think

Read the fiction book. Remember that this book is a made-up story. Choose from the activities listed below or make up some of your own.

1. Could there have been a dinosaur in your backyard millions of years ago?

2. How big was the dinosaur when he was hatched?

3. How big was the dinosaur when he was five years old?

4. Do you think dinosaurs ate lima beans? Why or why not?

5. What kind of dinosaur used to live in the boy's backyard?

6. Why could the dinosaur make the whole neighborhood shake?

7. Long ago, did the dinosaur live all by himself?

8. Why would dinosaurs seem like they are playing "Hide and Seek"?

9. Why would the dinosaurs fight?

10. Could dinosaurs have found shelter? Why or why not?

11. Could the little boy live in a swamp? Why or why not?

12. If you had a dinosaur in your backyard, what games would you play?

13. If you could talk to a dinosaur, what would you ask him?

14. If you could have a pet dinosaur, which one would you choose?

15. What would you name your pet dinosaur?

DINOSAURS

Directions: On the line below each dinosaur write FICTION if you would find the picture in a fiction book and NONFICTION if you would find the picture in a true book about dinosaurs.

Elephants

Living Things and Their Environments–1

TOPIC: ELEPHANTS
NONFICTION: *Elephant Families* by Arthur Dorros
FICTION: *But No Elephants* by Terry Smath

Nonfiction: Things to Make You Think

Read the nonfiction book. Remember that this is a true book and it is important to listen for the facts. Choose from the activities listed below or make up your own.

1. Describe how an elephant family is like your family. How are the families different?

2. How much does a grown elephant weigh?

3. How much does a grown elephant eat in a day?

4. What does a baby elephant eat?

5. Who is the leader of the elephant family? Why?

6. How are elephant feet special? Why is this important?

7. What can an elephant do with its trunk?

8. What can elephants do with their tusks?

9. How do elephants "talk long distance" to each other?

10. How do elephants say "hello" to old friends?

11. How do elephants breathe under water?

12. Are elephants always gray?

13. Why would people kill elephants?

14. Where do the two different kinds of elephants live?

15. How are the two kinds of elephants different?

16. Do you think it would be fun to ride on an elephant? Why?

Living Things and Their Environments-1

TOPIC: ELEPHANTS
NONFICTION: _Elephant Families_ by Arthur Dorros
FICTION: _But No Elephants_ by Terry Smath

Fiction: Things to Make You Think

Read the fiction book. Remember that this is a made-up story. Choose from the activities listed below or make up some of your own.

1. What is the first animal Grandma Tildy buys from the pet man?

2. What does the bird do that makes Grandma Tildy happy?

3. What animal does Grandma Tildy buy next?

4. How is the beaver helpful to Grandma Tildy?

5. The third time Grandma Tildy meets the pet man, what does she buy from him?

6. Who is "you-know-who"?

7. Grandma Tildy buys lots of animals but she does not want an elephant. Why do you think she does not want an elephant?

8. How does the woodpecker help Grandma Tildy?

9. Why does Grandma Tildy finally let the elephant come into the house?

10. What is the terrible crash that wakes everyone up?

11. Does Grandma have enough food for an elephant? From what you have read about elephants in the nonfiction book, why would it be impossible?

12. The elephant feels badly for causing so much trouble, so what does he finally think of doing to help them all?

13. What direction does he walk in?

14. Where do you think the animals are all living now?

15. Where would you go to escape winter? Find some places on a map.

ELEPHANTS

Directions: Label the parts of the elephant using the following words. Then color the elephant the way you would dress on Elmer's Special Day.

Word List:

trunk	ears	feet	tail	tusks
eyes	mouth	legs	nose	

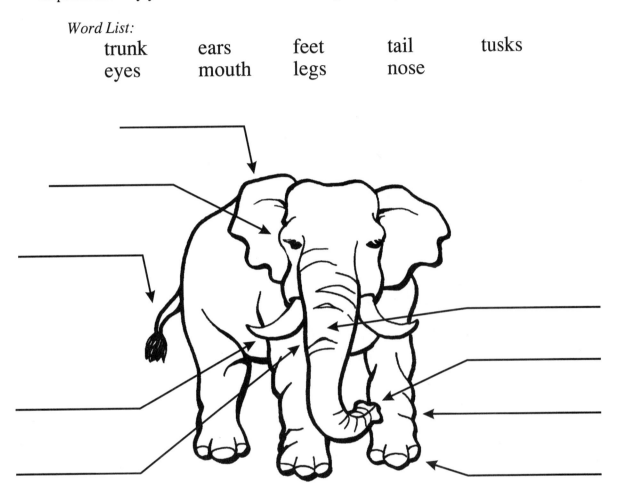

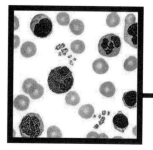

Germs

Human Body, Care–1

TOPIC: GERMS
NONFICTION: *Germs Make Me Sick* by Melvin Berger
FICTION: *Arthur's Chicken Pox* by Marc Brown

Nonfiction: Things to Make You Think

Read the nonfiction book. Remember that this is a true book and it is important to listen for the facts. Choose from the activities listed below or make up your own.

1. Can you see germs with just your eyes?

2. What instrument helps to see and study germs?

3. Are all germs harmful?

4. What protects our bodies from many germs?

5. Name some ways germs can get into our bodies.

6. What are the two kinds of blood cells?

7. Which kind of blood cell fights germs?

8. How do bacteria kill cells?

9. What carries poisons to other parts of your body?

10. Where do viruses multiply?

11. How does taking your blood help the doctor help you?

12. How does medicine help your body when you are attacked by bacteria?

13. Can medicine kill viruses?

14. How does getting a vaccination help you stay healthy?

15. Name some ways to help you stay healthy.

Human Body, Care–1

TOPIC: GERMS
NONFICTION: *Germs Make Me Sick* by Melvin Berger
FICTION: *Arthur's Chicken Pox* by Marc Brown

Fiction: Things to Make You Think

Read the fiction book. Remember that this book is a made-up story. Choose from the activities listed below or make up your own.

1. Have you ever had chicken pox? Tell or write about your experience or about someone you know who has had chicken pox.

2. Where is Arthur's family planning to go on Saturday?

3. Why does D.W. think Arthur is pretending?

4. How does D.W. know the next day that Arthur is really sick?

5. What does Muffy bring to Arthur?

6. How does Dad try to help Arthur?

7. Do you think D.W. is trying to make Arthur feel better? Why or why not?

8. How does D.W. make herself look sick?

9. Why does D.W. want to get chicken pox?

10. Why is Grandma Thora upset with D.W.?

11. How is D.W. "torturing" Arthur?

12. Why doesn't D.W. want Arthur to get well by Saturday?

13. What happens Saturday morning?

14. Why does Arthur start laughing? Do you think he is being mean?

15. Is chicken pox caused by bacteria or a virus?

GERMS

Directions: Make your own poster to remind you how to stay healthy. Post it in your room.

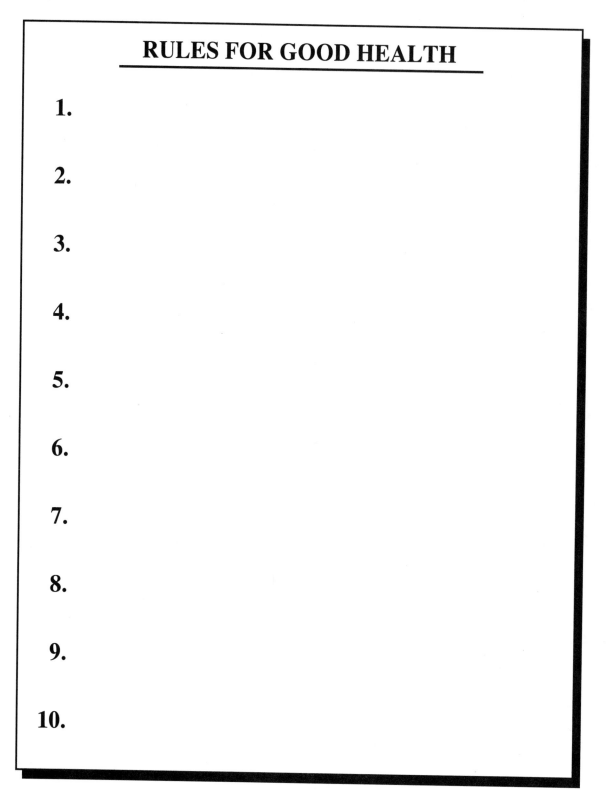

RULES FOR GOOD HEALTH

1.

2.

3.

4.

5.

6.

7.

8.

9.

10.

Milk

Living Things and Their Environment–1

TOPIC: MILK

NONFICTION: *Milk from Cow to Carton* by Aliki

FICTION: *Two Cool Cows* by Toby Speed

Nonfiction: Things to Make You Think

Read the nonfiction book. Remember that this is a true book and it is important to listen for the facts. Choose from the activities listed below or make up your own.

1. How many stomachs does a cow have?

2. Why do they need so many?

3. What is the "cud"?

4. Which stomach makes food into milk?

5. Why is the phrase "you are what you eat" important for a cow?

6. Why does the farmer wash the cow before milking her?

7. Does milking hurt the cow?

8. Why is the milk kept in a refrigerated tank?

9. What does the word "homogenized" mean?

10. When you go to the grocery store, count how many different kinds of milk are in the dairy case.

11. From where does the word "pasteurize" come?

12. Name as many things as you can that are made with milk.

13. What other animals give milk that people drink?

Living Things and Their Environment–1

TOPIC: MILK
NONFICTION: *Milk from Cow to Carton* by Aliki
FICTION: *Two Cool Cows* by Toby Speed

Fiction: Things to Make You Think

Read the fiction book. Remember that this book is a made-up story. Choose from the activities listed below or make up your own.

1. Can you recite the nursery rhyme "Hey Diddle Diddle"?

2. What are the names of the "two cool cows"?

3. Who do the black boots belong to?

4. Where is the best jumping-off place for the moon?

5. Find a surprised fish on the page where the cows are splashing through the buggity bog.

6. What are the cows looking for on the moon?

7. What are the names of the four Huckabuck kids?

8. Find the kids in the picture with the cows in the moon meadow. Where are they?

9. What are the cows eating on the moon?

10. Can anything really grow on the moon?

11. Would you like to live on Huckabuck Farm? Why or why not?

12. Make up a story about one or more of the following animals:

    a. two cool horses

    b. two cool dogs

    c. two cool cats

    d. two cool monkeys

MILK

Directions: Color the rhyming pairs of cows. Use a different color for each pair.

Rocks

The Earth, Rocks, and Minerals–1

TOPIC: ROCKS

NONFICTION: *Let's Go Rock Collecting* by Roma Gans

FICTION: *The Rock* by Peter Parnall

Nonfiction: Things to Make You Think

Read the nonfiction book. Remember that this is a true book and it is important to listen for the facts. Choose from the activities listed below or make up your own.

1. How old are rocks?

2. Why are rocks used to build things?

3. What is the Earth's crust made of?

4. What does "igneous" mean?

5. What is magma?

6. What is lava?

7. Name two igneous rocks.

8. Name two sedimentary rocks.

9. Name four metamorphic rocks.

10. What changes rocks over the years into metamorphic rocks?

11. Where is marble used in homes and buildings?

12. Look around your neighborhood, on your way to school, or anywhere you travel for ways that rocks are used besides roads and cement. How many ways can you see or think of?

13. Rock collecting is great fun. Start your collection today!

The Earth, Rocks, and Minerals–1

TOPIC: ROCKS

NONFICTION: *Let's Go Rock Collecting* by Roma Gans

FICTION: *The Rock* by Peter Parnall

Fiction: Things to Make You Think

Read the fiction book. Remember that this is a made-up story. Choose from the activities listed below or make up your own.

1. Why do the Indians wait for the deer to come to the pond?

2. Why can the fox get into the deep den and the boy can't?

3. What is another word for "crevice"?

4. What is the meaning of "fragile"?

5. Who finds a home in the rotted tree?

6. Why is the rock armor for the mouse?

7. Why don't Moose or Hawk return to the Rock?

8. How is the fire good for the Rock and the tree and the forest?

9. Pretend you are the Rock. What would you tell the people and the animals that visit the forest?

10. The Indian in the Rock sees many things over the years. How do you think he feels when the fire is raging all around him?

11. Is a forest fire hot enough to melt a rock?

12. Design something made out of rock. Draw a picture of it. Give it a special name. Build a model if you can.

ROCKS

Directions: Circle words from the books in the puzzle below. Use the following word list:

rocks   fox
magma   den
lava   crevice
igneous   fire
marble   melt

```
B  H  D  E  N  V  A  L  T  P
R  O  C  K  S  F  I  R  E  N
H  O  S  N  M  A  F  O  X  J
I  G  N  E  O  U  S  S  V  M
T  R  M  A  R  B  L  E  B  F
V  E  L  A  V  A  M  E  L  T
C  R  E  V  I  C  E  G  O  P
M  A  G  M  A  H  A  C  W  T
```

Snakes

Living Things and Their Environments–1

TOPIC: SNAKES
NONFICTION: *Snakes Are Hunters* by Patricia Lauber
FICTION: *Verdi* by Canon

Nonfiction: Things to Make You Think

Read the nonfiction book. Remember that this is a true book and it is important to listen for the facts. Choose from the activities listed below or make up your own.

1. Why do you think the snake is smiling on the cover of the book?

2. Where is the Young Explorers Club going to learn about snakes?

3. How many different kinds of snakes are there?

4. Lie down on the floor, keeping your hands by your sides and your legs together. Try to move like a snake as described in the book. Try to hold your eyes open while doing this, just as a snake does.

5. How do snakes know something nearby is moving?

6. Could you swallow a frog whole, as a snake does? Why not?

7. Do all snakes kill their prey before they eat it?

8. Are all snakes poisonous?

9. What animals are enemies of snakes?

10. Why does a snake have to shed its skin?

11. List all the ways snakes are alike:

   a. _____   f. _____

   b. _____   g. _____

   c. _____   h. _____

   d. _____   i. _____

   e. _____   j. _____

Living Things and Their Environments–1

TOPIC: SNAKES
NONFICTION: *Snakes Are Hunters* by Patricia Lauber
FICTION: *Verdi* by Canon

Fiction: Things to Make You Think

Read the fiction book. Remember that this is a made-up story even though it is based on real happenings. Choose from the activities listed below or make up your own.

1. What kind of a snake is Verdi?

2. How is Verdi different from Umbles, Aggie, and Ribbon?

3. What does Verdi think about the "Greens"?

4. Why does Verdi want to stay yellow?

5. Would you like to pretend you are an arrow, like Verdi does? Why or why not?

6. Why are the "Greens" worried about Verdi?

7. Why is Verdi upset when his skin starts to peel?

8. Why does Verdi leave the mud on?

9. What does Verdi forget about when he launches himself from the treetop?

10. How do the "Greens" help Verdi after he falls?

11. How many animals can you find in the big double-page picture?

13. Why can't the other animals see Verdi as he watches the moon?

13. Can Verdi or any other living things stop themselves from growing?

14. Fold a piece of paper in half and then in half again. Number the sections 1, 2, 3, and 4. Show the stages of Verdi's life: birth, yellow stage, molting, and adult.

15. Pick another animal and write or tell a story about how it does not want to grow up.

SNAKES

Directions: Color the real snake to look like one of the snakes in the true book. Color the other snake to look like a make-believe snake. Make up your own story about it.

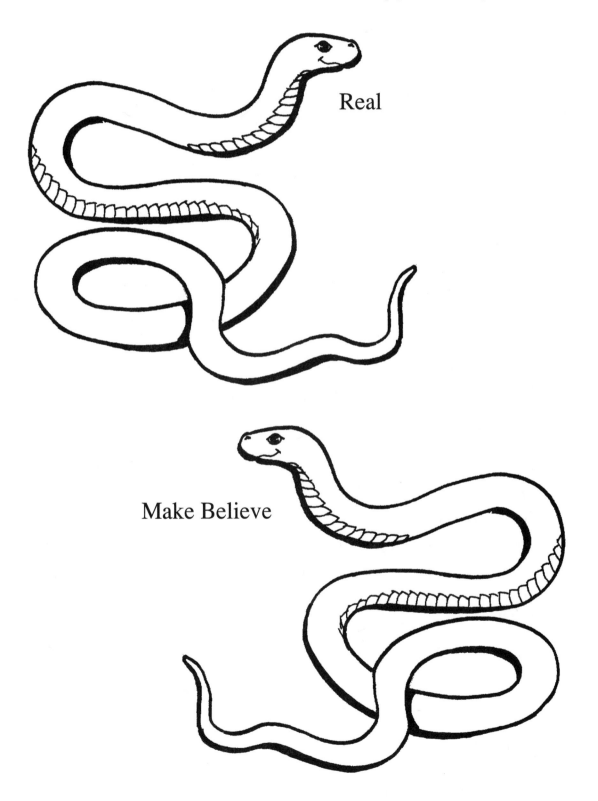

Real

Make Believe

Thunderstorms

Electricity–1

TOPIC: THUNDERSTORMS
NONFICTION: *Flash, Crash, Rumble and Roll* by Franklyn M. Branley
FICTION: *Thunder Cake* by Patricia Polacco

Nonfiction: Things to Make You Think

Read the nonfiction book. Remember that this is a true book and it is important to listen for the facts. Choose from the activities listed below or make up your own.

1. Why won't the sailboat move?

2. How do the people know a thunderstorm is coming?

3. What is carried up into the clouds by the warm air?

4. When the water vapor cools up in the clouds, what do the clouds become?

5. Why do airplanes stay out of thunderclouds?

6. What carries electricity through the air?

7. Does all thunder sound alike? Can you make some thunder noises?

8. Which comes first, thunder or lightning?

9. Make some sound waves. Can you see them?

10. Which travels faster, light or sound?

11. How can you tell how far away a storm is?

12. Why do you have to be careful when it is lightning?

13. Where are some safe places to be during a storm?

14. Why do you think people long ago feared thunder and lightning so much?

Electricity–1

TOPIC: THUNDERSTORMS
NONFICTION: *Flash, Crash, Rumble and Roll* by Franklyn M. Branley
FICTION: *Thunder Cake* by Patricia Polacco

Fiction: Things to Make You Think

Read the fiction book. Remember that this book is a made-up story. Choose from the activities listed below or make up your own.

1. What is the Russian word for "Grandmother"?

2. How does Babushka know a storm is coming?

3. Why is the little girl hiding under the bed?

4. What does Grandmother need to know to make "real" Thunder Cake?

5. Why is Patricia afraid of old Nellie Peck Hen?

6. Why is Patricia afraid of old Kick Cow?

7. What do Babushka and Patricia need to get from the dry shed?

8. What are the secret ingredients of Thunder Cake?

9. What four things does Patricia do that show she is very brave?

10. What flavor is the Thunder Cake?

11. Does Babushka understand about lightning and thunder?

12. Try making your own Thunder Cake from the recipe at the back of the book.

13. Do you have a special memory about something you have done with a grandmother or grandfather? Write or tell about it.

14. Why do you think Patricia is no longer afraid of thunder?

THUNDERSTORMS

Directions: Some activities are safe to do during a thunderstorm. Others are not! Write the words "safe" or "unsafe" under each picture to show you know what to do during a thunderstorm.

Volcanoes

The Earth–1

TOPIC: VOLCANOES
NONFICTION: *Volcanoes* by Franklyn M. Branley
FICTION: *Hill of Fire* by Thomas P. Lewis

Nonfiction: Things to Make You Think

Read the nonfiction book. Remember that this is a true book and it is important to listen for the facts. Choose from the activities listed below or make up your own.

1. When Mount Tambora blew its top in 1815, it caused a huge change in the normal weather patterns in the New England states. Explain what happened and why.

2. What causes an earthquake?

3. Find Mt. Vesuvius on a map. What country is it in?

4. Find Indonesia on a map.

5. Explain how the top of Mt. St. Helens was blown off.

6. How are earthquakes and volcanoes related?

7. What is the Ring of Fire and why do you think it is named that?

8 Why is Hawaii such a unique place geologically?

9. Pretend that you are the son or daughter of Dionisio Pulido. Write a paragraph about the day "the field became a mountain."

10. Our Earth is always changing. Retell or rewrite the explanation in your own words of how volcanoes and earthquakes change our Earth.

11. Define "plates."

12. Find Paricutin, Mexico, on a map. Then look at the map in the book. What two plates moving caused the volcano mountain to form on Donisio Pulido's farm?

The Earth–1

TOPIC: VOLCANOES
NONFICTION: *Volcanoes* by Franklyn M. Branley
FICTION: *Hill of Fire* by Thomas P. Lewis

Fiction: Things to Make You Think

Read the fiction book. Remember that this book is a made-up story. Choose from the activities listed below or make up your own.

1. In what country does the farmer live?

2. Why is the farmer unhappy?

3. Where does the farmer go very early in the morning, every morning?

4. What do you think the farmer wants to happen?

5. Do you think the ox is always helpful? Why or why not?

6. Why does the ox lie down in the middle of the field?

7. Why does Pablo go to the field?

8. What is coming out of the hole in the ground made by the plow?

9. Why do Pablo, the farmer, and the ox all run away?

10. Why does the farmer ring the old church bell?

11. What is making the loud booming sounds?

12. What is the "hill of fire"?

13. Why do the soldiers come to the village?

14. What does "El Monstruo" mean in English?

15. How do you think the volcano helps the people of the village?

VOLCANOES

Directions: Draw a volcano. Use the words in the list below to label its parts.

Word List:

conduit   lava flow   magma   chamber
crater   central   vent   gas and dust

Whales

Living Things and Their Environment–1

TOPIC: WHALES
NONFICTION: *Whales* by Gail Gibbons
FICTION: *Rainbow Fish and the Big Blue Whale* by Marcus Pfister

Nonfiction: Things to Make You Think

Read the nonfiction book. Remember that this is a true book and it is important to listen for the facts. Choose from the activities listed below or make up your own.

1. Are whales fish?

2. Are all whales huge?

3. What animal do you know that looks like the ancient mesonychid?

4. What is the purpose of blubber?

5. How do scientists know that the ancestor of the whale probably walked on four legs?

6. What is a fluke?

7. Do flippers help the whale move?

8. We have nostrils. What is the name given to the whales' "nostrils"?

9. How does the whale find his way when he cannot see?

10. How do whales "talk" to each other?

11. What do you call a group of whales traveling together?

12. What other animal has bulls, cows, and calves?

13. Name each kind of whale in the book and one special feature of each.

14. Why are there laws about killing whales now?

15. Choose your favorite whale story and read more.

Living Things and Their Environment–1

TOPIC: WHALES

NONFICTION: *Whales* by Gail Gibbons

FICTION: *Rainbow Fish and the Big Blue Whale* by Marcus Pfister

Fiction: Things to Make You Think

Read the fiction book. Remember that this book is a made-up story. Choose from the activities listed below or make up your own.

1. How many friends of Rainbow Fish can you count in the first picture?

2. What other sea creatures do you see in the first picture?

3. What is another name for "krill"?

4. Why does the big blue whale like the same spot in the ocean as Rainbow Fish and his friends?

5. The fish with the jagged fins is in a bad mood. How does that effect the other fish?

6. Do you think the whale could eat all the krill?

7. Why does the whale lash out and scare all the little fish?

8. Where does the Rainbow Fish go for safety to hide from the whale?

9. Could the Rainbow Fish have stayed in the cave forever? Why or why not?

10. What happens to the krill?

11. Rainbow Fish is very wise and very brave. How does he solve the problem with the whale? Is it a good idea?

12. What is the misunderstanding all about?

13. How could the fight have been avoided from the very beginning?

14. Choose your favorite fish and draw a picture of it. Use tin foil to make the glittering scales.

Grade

Ants

Insects–2

TOPIC: ANTS
NONFICTION: *Ant Cities* by Arthur Dorros
FICTION: *Two Bad Ants* by Chris Van Allsburg

Nonfiction: Things to Make You Think

Read the nonfiction book. Remember that this is a true book and it is important to listen for the facts. Choose from the activities listed or make up your own.

1. Why do ants build hills?

2. What is the place inside the hill where the ants live called?

3. What are the ants that build the nest called?

4. How does building a hill make the ant home perfect for all kinds of weather?

5. Why is the ant home like a city?

6. What else does the worker ant do besides build tunnels and rooms?

7. What does the queen ant do?

8. What is the special name for a baby ant?

9. Explain the jobs of each type of ant:

   a. queen

   b. worker

   c. new queen

   d. male

10. Could one ant live alone for very long? Why or why not?

11. Why do you think the ant city can have so many thousands of ants living together?

12. How do ants hunt for food?

13. Where are some places you could look for ants?

14. Try building your own ant farm. The directions are on the last page of the book.

15. You can make your own ant picture using a stamp pad and your thumb or finger-print. An ant has three body parts, six legs, and two antennas.

Insects–2

TOPIC: ANTS

NONFICTION: *Ant Cities* by Arthur Dorros

FICTION: *Two Bad Ants* by Chris Van Allsburg

Fiction: Things to Make You Think

Read the fiction book. Remember that this is a made-up story. Choose from the activities listed below or make up your own.

1. What is the ant carrying?

2. Why do the ants want to keep the queen happy?

3. Why are the ants willing to go on the "long and dangerous journey"?

4. What is the "forest" made of?

5. What is the mountain made of?

6. What is this "strange place" the ants have entered?

7. Why do you think the ants are nervous?

8. What are the "sparkling crystals" really?

9. Where do the "two bad ants" sleep that night?

10. Why are they bad?

11. What is the "boiling brown lake" really?

12. What is the "chamber" called that was spinning the "two bad ants"?

13. The artist, Chris Van Allsburg, used a pencil to draw many of the pictures in the book. Choose your favorite picture and try to draw it yourself with just your pencil.

14. Think of some other places or equipment in the kitchen in which the two bad ants could get into trouble.

15. Have you ever been separated from the group you were with? What happened during that time? Tell or write a story about your adventure.

ANTS

Directions: List the things that help you tell the difference between the fiction book and the nonfiction book. See the example.

Example: Talking ants / Worker ants

Fiction   *Nonfiction*

_____   _____

_____   _____

_____   _____

_____   _____

_____   _____

_____   _____

_____   _____

_____   _____

Bees and Bugs

Insects–2

TOPIC: BEES AND BUGS
NONFICTION: *Bugs and Other Insects* by Bobbie Kalman
FICTION: *The Bee Tree* by Patricia Polacco

Nonfiction: Things to Make You Think

Read the nonfiction book. Remember that this is a true book and it is important to listen for the facts. Choose from the activities listed below or make up your own.

1. Are all insects bugs?

2. What are spiracles?

3. Explain the difference between compound and single eyes.

4. Draw your own picture to explain "complete metamorphosis."

5. Why would animals stay away from and not eat a bright-colored insect?

6. How can you make a sound like a grasshopper?

7. How are insects helpful?

8. Why haven't all the insects been discovered?

9. Make your own insect tree like the one in the book.

10. How are insects all alike?

11. What is the "elytra" and how is it helpful?

12. How are the stinging actions of the wasp and the bee different?

13. List the four differences between the moth and the butterfly.

14. Why do we kill houseflies?

15. Does the grasshopper get upset when it loses a leg? Why or why not?

16. Check up on yourself at the end of the book. How much did you learn?

Insects–2

TOPIC: BEES AND BUGS

NONFICTION: *Bugs and Other Insects* by Bobbie Kalman

FICTION: *The Bee Tree* by Patricia Polacco

Fiction: Things to Make You Think

Read the fiction book. Remember that this book is a made-up story. Choose from the activities listed below or make up your own.

1. Look carefully at the first picture. What is the blue item in the lower right-hand corner? If you are not sure, ask an adult.

2. Why is the cat smiling?

3. Why is Grampa so careful not to hurt the bees?

4. Would it be hard to follow a bee? Why?

5. Do you think the bee knows he is being followed?

6. Do you think the Hermann Sisters will be able to keep up the chase?

7. How many vehicles are in the picture with Bertha Fitchworth?

8. Why does Grampa let out another bee?

9. What instruments are the traveling musicians playing?

10. How can you tell that Baby Sylvester is having fun?

11. Who lets the third bee out of the jar?

12. Why do the girls need damp leaves for the fire?

13. How do the girls use the clean diaper?

14. What does Mary Ellen learn by going to the bee tree?

15. How is chasing knowledge like chasing a bee?

Body Human

Human Body–Grade 2

TOPIC: BODY HUMAN
NONFICTION: *I Can Read About My Own Body* by David Eastman
FICTION: *The Shortest Kid in the World* by Corinne Demas Bliss

Nonfiction: Things to Make You Think

Read the nonfiction book. Remember that this is a true book and it is important to listen for the facts. Choose from the activities listed below or make up your own.

1. The systems of your body work together like a team. Name the systems.

2. How many bones are there in your skeletal system?

3. Bones are living. What keeps them alive and able to grow and repair themselves?

4. Name the three kinds of joints and give an example of each.

5. How many muscles are there in your body?

6. Name the two kinds of muscles and give an example of each.

7. Digestion takes place in several places. Name them.

8. Why can you swallow food even if you are standing on your head?

9. How does food get into your bloodstream?

10. How does oxygen get into your bloodstream?

11. What is the job of the circulatory system?

12. What is the job of the arteries and veins?

13. What is the job of the red blood cells, white blood cells, and platelets?

14. What are the three main parts of the nervous system?

15. The skin is like wrapping paper that protects all the systems. Name the two layers.

Human Body–Grade 2

TOPIC: BODY HUMAN
NONFICTION: *I Can Read About My Own Body* by David Eastman
FICTION: *The Shortest Kid in the World* by Corinne Demas Bliss

Fiction: Things to Make You Think

Read the fiction book. Remember that this book is a made-up story. Choose from the activities listed below or make up your own.

1. Why isn't Emily's mother worried about Emily being short?

2. What does Emily do to try to grow faster?

3. What is different about the way Marietta handles being short compared to how Emily does?

4. Do you think Emily wants to be the shortest again? Why?

5. Why does Emily stop eating spinach and doing her stretching exercises?

6. How does Marietta help Emily feel better about her body?

7. Does everyone grow at the same rate?

8. Does it matter whether you are short or tall or medium or small? Why or why not?

9. What might be some reasons why we all have different bodies?

10. What might be some reasons why we grow at different rates?

11. Look at class pictures from past years. Can you tell how your friends have changed throughout the years? Describe some of the changes you notice.

12. Compare pictures of your brothers or sisters with yourself at different ages. Have you all grown at the same rate?

BODY HUMAN

Directions: Look at the people in the pictures. On the line below each picture write FICTION if the character would be in the fiction book. Write NONFICTION if the picture would be found in a true book.

Bugs

Insects–2

TOPIC: BUGS

NONFICTION: *Bugs! Bugs! Bugs!* by Jennifer Dussling

FICTION: *I Know an Old Lady Who Swallowed a Fly* by Nadine Bernard Westcott

Nonfiction: Things to Make You Think

Read the nonfiction book. Remember that this is a true book and it is important to listen for the facts. Choose from the activities listed below or make up your own.

1. Which bug do you think is the scariest?

2. What is a bug's worst enemy?

3. What does the praying mantis look like? How does camouflage help it?

4. A grasshopper is only about two inches long. How long do you think the wood ant is?

5. How does the wood ant kill its prey?

6. What is the picture in the rock called?

7. Could you eat 250 hot dogs in one day? Why do you think the dragonfly can eat so much?

8. Which bug is a little scary to people? Why?

9. What is an assassin?

10. What do male stag beetles fight about?

11. Bugs can be really nasty. How do the following bugs protect themselves?

    a. stinkbug

    b. monarch butterfly

    c. tropical lappet moth caterpillar

    d. postman butterfly caterpillar

    e. thorn bug

    f. click bug

12. There are interesting bug facts in the book. Can you add some of your own? Try the encyclopedia or the 595.715 section of your library.

Insects–2

TOPIC: BUGS

NONFICTION: *Bugs! Bugs! Bugs!* by Jennifer Dussling

FICTION: *I Know an Old Lady Who Swallowed a Fly* by Nadine Bernard Westcott

Fiction: Things to Make You Think

Read the fiction book. Remember that this book is a made-up story. Choose from the activities listed below or make up your own.

1. What is the old lady eating when she swallows the fly?

2. The cat also has a problem with a fly. What is it?

3. What happens when the old lady swallows the fly?

4. What does the cat have on his head?

5. What is the old lady using? Why?

6. Would swallowing a fly kill you?

7. What is the old lady doing in the picture that could kill her?

8. Does she swallow the spider on purpose?

9. Find the dog and the cat in the picture. Where are they?

10. What part of the bird does the old lady have trouble swallowing?

11. What is the old lady cooking? Is the cat worried? Why?

12. Does she use her own cat?

13. Does she use her own dog?

14. How is she able to catch the goat?

15. Why do you think the sofa breaks?

16. She causes a lot of problems in the neighborhood. Why?

17. Sing or play the song. It is easy to memorize.

BUGS

Directions: Number the animals in the order that the old lady swallows them. Put the number on the line below the animal.

Caterpillar to Butterfly

Life Cycles–2

TOPIC: CATERPILLAR TO BUTTERFLY
NONFICTION: *From Caterpillar to Butterfly* by Deborah Heiligman
FICTION: *The Very Hungry Caterpillar* by Eric Carle

Nonfiction: Things to Make You Think

Read the nonfiction book. Remember that this is a true book and it is important to listen for the facts. Choose from the activities listed below or make up your own.

1. How does the caterpillar begin life?

2. Where does the mother butterfly lay the egg?

3. How big is the egg?

4. What does the tiny caterpillar eat?

5. What is another name for the caterpillar?

6. How long does the caterpillar eat and eat and eat?

7. What is molting?

8. The last time a caterpillar molts it develops a hard shell. What is it called?

9. How long do the kids have to wait for the chrysalis to open?

10. The butterfly is wet and crumpled when it breaks out of the chrysalis. What has to happen before the butterfly can fly?

11. Why do the students have to let the butterfly go?

12. Why do the kids feel a little sad and a little happy?

13. What will happen if the butterfly is a female?

14. This circle of life has another name. What is it?

15. Which is your favorite butterfly at the end of the book?

Life Cycles–2

TOPIC: CATERPILLAR TO BUTTERFLY
NONFICTION: *From Caterpillar to Butterfly* by Deborah Heiligman
FICTION: *The Very Hungry Caterpillar* by Eric Carle

Fiction: Things to Make You Think

Read the fiction book. Remember that this book is a made-up story. Choose from the activities listed below or make up some of your own.

1. Where is the egg in the picture? Can you find it?

2. Look carefully at the picture of the moon. What do you see?

3. What happens on Sunday?

4. What is the caterpillar looking for?

5. What does the caterpillar do on Monday?

6. What fruit does he eat through on Tuesday?

7. What does he eat through on Wednesday?

8. What happens on Thursday?

9. Is he still hungry?

10. What does he do on Friday?

11. Can you name all the things he eats on Saturday?

12. What makes the caterpillar feel better after he eats all that food?

13. Why does he grow so big?

14. What happens to the caterpillar?

15. What happens after the cocoon opens?

CATERPILLAR TO BUTTERFLY

Directions: Color your own butterfly. It can be real or make believe.

Digest This!

Human Body, Digestive System–2

TOPIC: DIGEST THIS!

NONFICTION: *The Digestive System* by Darlene R. Stille

FICTION: *The Berenstain Bears and Too Much Junk Food* by Stan Berenstain and Jan Berenstain

Nonfiction: Things to Make You Think

Read the nonfiction book. Remember that this is a true book and it is important to listen for the facts. Choose from the activities listed below or make up your own.

1. What does the word "digest" mean?

2. What is the first step in digestion?

3. How does saliva help?

4. What is the tube that helps food travel from the mouth to the stomach?

5. What is the "bag of muscles" called?

6. How does the stomach "go to work" on the food you eat?

7. When food leaves the stomach, what does it look like?

8. Measure out 20 feet so you can see how long the small intestine really is.

9. Tiny food particles or pieces leave the small intestine and enter what part?

10. How do our bodies get energy from the food we eat?

11. Which is longer, the large intestine or the small intestine?

12. What happens to parts of the food that our bodies cannot use?

13. How do the liver and gallbladder help digestion?

14. How did doctors long ago find out about the digestive system?

15. List four ways to be sure you are keeping your digestive system healthy.

Human Body, Digestive System–2

TOPIC: DIGEST THIS!
NONFICTION: *The Digestive System* by Darlene R. Stille
FICTION: *The Berenstain Bears and Too Much Junk Food* by Stan Berenstain and Jan Berenstain

Fiction: Things to Make You Think

Read the fiction book. Remember that this book is a made-up story. Choose from the activities listed below or make up some of your own.

1. What does Mama Bear notice about Brother and Sister Bear?

2. What does she decide to do about it?

3. How does Papa know he has to stop eating so many sweets?

4. What drinks are healthier than soda pop?

5. What are some of the sensible foods the Bear Family buys at the store?

6. Who does Mama Bear meet in the check out line?

7. Why does Dr. Grizzly want to see the Bear Family at his office?

8. How do we know what our insides look like?

9. Name some of the body's organs.

10. What is it called when organs all work together?

11. Why does Dr. Grizzly show the Bears slides of different foods?

12. What harm does junk food do?

13. What else do we have to do to stay healthy besides eat healthy food?

14. How do you exercise?

15. What are your favorite healthy snacks?

Fireflies

Insects–2

TOPIC: FIREFLIES
NONFICTION: *Fireflies in the Night* by Judy Hawes
FICTION: *Fireflies!* by Julie Brinckloe

Nonfiction: Things to Make You Think

Read the nonfiction book. Remember that this is a true book and it is important to listen for the facts. Choose from the activities listed below or make up some of your own.

1. What time of year do we usually see fireflies?

2. Is there another name for fireflies?

3. What insect family do they belong to?

4. Can baby fireflies fly?

5. How do you make fireflies glow brighter? How do you make them dimmer?

6. How do people in the Caribbean use fireflies?

7. If you could catch enough fireflies to make a lantern, where would you put it to make good use of the light?

8. Have you seen other beetles? What are some other kinds?

9. Where in the world do they use fireflies to light gardens?

10. How can fireflies make "cold" light?

11. How do fireflies "talk" to each other?

12. Why do you think Grandma lets the fireflies go?

Insects–2

TOPIC: FIREFLIES
NONFICTION: *Fireflies in the Night* by Judy Hawes
FICTION: *Fireflies!* by Julie Brinckloe

Fiction: Things to Make You Think

Read the fiction book. Remember that this is a made-up story. Choose from the activities listed below or make up some of your own.

1. Why do you think the boy will not go out to his tree house?

2. What is the family having for dinner?

3. How do you know the boy is in a hurry?

4. Do you think he is excited about the flash he sees?

5. What would be a better and safer way to poke holes in the jar lid?

6. Why do you think it is so much fun to catch fireflies?

7. Why do the kids stop?

8. Why do the fireflies beat their wings against the sides of the jar and fall to the bottom of the jar?

9. Why does the boy cover his head with the covers?

10. Tell or write a story about when you hunted fireflies.

11. Pretend you are a firefly and you have been captured and are living in a jar. Tell or write a story about how you feel.

12. Why does the little boy have a tear in his eye and a smile on his face at the same time?

13. Do you think the boy does the right thing? What would you do?

FIREFLIES

Directions: Cut out the pattern of a jar. Trace around it to make more jars. Write the following vocabulary words on the jars. Place them in alphabetical order. They can also be used as flash cards or to make up your own game.

beetles	wings	jungle	cornfield	lanterns	candle
chemicals	signals	fireflies	jar	breathe	scissors

Food

Human Body, Digestion–2

TOPIC: FOOD

NONFICTION: *What Happens to a Hamburger?* by Paul Showers

FICTION: *Gregory, the Terrible Eater* by Mitchell Sharmat

Nonfiction: Things to Make You Think

Read the nonfiction book. Remember that this is a true book and it is important to listen for the facts. Choose from the activities listed below or make up your own.

1. Do you like to eat? What do you like best?

2. What would you be like if you didn't have any energy? Have you ever felt that way? Tell or write about what happened.

3. Does the sugar really disappear?

4. Try the experiment. Be sure you are alone when you do this. It is gross to watch!

5. What kinds of food make your mouth "water"?

6. What is the epiglottis?

7. Can you still swallow when you are standing on your head?

8. Explain how the stomach helps digestion.

9. What is the difference between the small and large intestines?

10. What is a molecule?

11. How long does it usually take to digest your food?

Human Body, Digestion–2

TOPIC: FOOD
NONFICTION: *What Happens to a Hamburger?* by Paul Showers
FICTION: *Gregory, the Terrible Eater* by Mitchell Sharmat

Fiction: Things to Make You Think

Read the fiction book. Remember that this book is a made-up story. Choose from the activities listed below or make up your own.

1. Why does Gregory think he is an average goat?

2. What makes him not average?

3. Is Gregory a picky eater?

4. Have you ever felt like Gregory?

5. If Gregory doesn't eat, what will happen to him?

6. What kind of food does Gregory want?

7. Why do Mother and Father Goat think Gregory's favorite foods are "revolting"?

8. What is Gregory dreaming of as he is excused from the table?

9. Why do Mother and Father Goat decide to take Gregory to the doctor?

10. Is the doctor's idea a good one? Do you have a better idea to help?

11. What is Gregory's favorite food?

12. Gregory does learn to like everything, and he is beginning to eat everything. Why does this become a problem for Gregory? Why would this be a problem for you?

13. Do Mother and Father Goat know what will happen if Gregory eats too much junk?

14. What is so good about breakfast the next morning?

15. What would be a balanced meal for you?

FOOD

Directions: Cut out the food pictures and group them with foods that go together. Make up some healthy meals that you like.

Growing Gardens

Seasons and Life Processes–2

TOPIC: GROWING GARDENS
NONFICTION: *The Reason for a Flower* by Ruth Heller
FICTION: *Inch by Inch: The Garden Song* by David Mallett

Nonfiction: Things to Make You Think

Read the nonfiction book. Remember that this is a true book and it is important to listen for the facts. Choose from the activities listed below or make up your own.

1. Birds and bees and butterflies do an important job for flowers. What is it?

2. Pollen travels in many ways. Name two.

3. What is an anther?

4. What is a stamen?

5. What is a style?

6. The flower can make seeds. Are all seeds alike? Look at some seeds in the fruit you have at home. Be sure to ask for help.

7. Name other ways seeds travel.

8. Seeds need three things to grow. Name them.

9. Animals that eat plants are called _____. Name some of your favorite ones.

10. Some plants eat meat. Any plant or animal that eats meat is _____.

11. Why is the rafflesia so interesting?

12. What flower may have been around when the dinosaurs were here?

13. "Grecian" means that the word "angiosperm" came from what language?

14. Research interesting flowers and plants you have never heard of. Learn about five new flowers or plants. Draw pictures of your newly found knowledge.

Seasons and Life Processes–2

TOPIC: GROWING GARDENS
NONFICTION: *Inch by Inch: The Garden Song* by David Mallett
FICTION: *The Reason for a Flower* by Ruth Heller

Fiction: Things to Make You Think

Read the fiction book. Remember that this book is a made-up story. Choose from the activities listed below or make up your own.

1. Why do you think the book is titled *Inch by Inch*?

2. Tell about a time you when have planted or helped plant something. What happened?

3. Why is the little boy so happy?

4. What does "fertile ground" mean?

5. What does the word "sow" mean?

6. Why is the boy praying for rain?

7. How can pulling weeds and picking up stones help the garden grow?

8. What is "nature's chain"?

9. Do you hear "music from the land"? Do what the boy is doing and listen carefully to the sounds of nature.

10. Why plant rows straight and long?

11. Why do we call our planet "Mother Earth"?

12. Why is the boy shaking his fist at the crow?

13. Have someone play the song for you or listen to the tape.

14. Try to write your own verse to the song.

15. See if you can name the fruits and vegetables on the last page.

GROWING GARDENS

Directions: Label the fruits and vegetables in the pictures.

Word List:

    corn, beets, apple, tomato, peppers, lemon, cherry, onion, carrot, eggplant, pear, strawberry, grapes

_____ _____ _____ _____

_____ _____ _____ _____

_____ _____ _____ _____

_____

Rain Forest

Water Cycle–2

TOPIC: RAIN FOREST
NONFICTION: *One Day in the Tropical Rain Forest* by Jean C. George
FICTION: *The Great Kapok Tree* by Lynne Cherry

Nonfiction: Things to Make You Think

Read the nonfiction book. Remember that this is a true book and it is important to listen for the facts. Choose from the activities listed below or make up your own.

1. Tepui lives near what river? Can you find it on a map of Venezuela?

2. What is a great Kiskadee?

3. What does "The mother was an apartment house" mean?

4. What is Dr. Juan Rivero's job?

5. Look at a globe. Find the Tropic of Cancer and the Tropic of Capricorn.

6. Why is the jaguar afraid of the ants?

7. What is a Coco do Mono?

8. What is a herpetologist?

9. What is the only thing that could save this rain forest?

10. Why are the plants always at war in the rain forest?

11. The rain forest gets 30 feet of water a year. Mark off 30 feet to see how much that is.

12. Why do the 11 bulldozers, 4 trucks, and 20 chain saw operators have to stop and wait?

13. What happens to the jaguar cub?

14. Why do Tepui and Dr. Rivero climb to the top of the tree?

15. How does the great Kiskadee help Dr. Rivero catch the nameless butterfly?

Water Cycle–2

TOPIC: RAIN FOREST

NONFICTION: *One Day in the Tropical Rain Forest* by Jean C. George

FICTION: *The Great Kapok Tree* by Lynne Cherry

Fiction: Things to Make You Think

Read the fiction book. Remember that this book is a made-up story. Choose from the activities listed below or make up your own.

1. Look carefully at the picture of the man trying to chop down the tree. What animals can you find hiding in the forest?

2. The boa constrictor does not harm the man. Why not?

3. Why does the bee not want the man to chop down the tree?

4. The monkeys explain to the man what will happen in the future if he cuts down the tree. Can you explain it to someone?

5. Draw a picture of what the birds see when the trees are cut down.

6. Count the number of frogs that ask the man not to chop down the tree.

7. The jaguar is worried about himself. Why?

8. Tree porcupines tell the man that we all need what trees produce. What is that?

9. Why does "what happens tomorrow depend on what you do today"? Can you give other examples?

10. The three-toed sloth lives in what layer of the rain forest?

11. The animals and the boy understand the importance of the rain forest. Do you? Does the man at the beginning of the story? Does he at the end of the story?

12. Pick your favorite animal of the rain forest. Find out more about it at the library.

13. Why would the man's boss want him to cut down the tree?

14. Name the layers of the rain forest.

15. Name the continents and islands where one can find rain forests.

RAIN FOREST

Directions: Put the following words in alphabetical order:

canopy	understory	rainfall	trees
insects	birds	lizards	plants
scientists	snakes	equator	humid

_____

_____

_____

_____

_____

_____

_____

_____

_____

_____

Rain, Rain Go Away

Water Cycle–2

TOPIC: RAIN, RAIN GO AWAY
NONFICTION: *Read About Weather* by Herta S. Breiter
FICTION: *It's Raining, It's Pouring* by Kin Eagle

Nonfiction: Things to Make You Think

Read the nonfiction book. Remember that this is a true book and it is important to listen for the facts. Choose from the activities listed below or make up your own.

1. Explain how wind is caused.

2. Look at the pictures of the numbered forces. What force would make it a good day to fly a kite?

3. What force would be good for a sailboat ride?

4. What force would be good for a football game?

5. Explain evaporation in your own words. Put a little water in a dish or glass. Record how long it takes for the water to evaporate.

6. Explain condensation in your own words. Can you make a glass "sweat"? Pour something ice cold into a glass on a hot day. What happens?

7. How are land fog and sea fog alike? How are they different?

8. Use cotton balls to create your own altocumulus, stratocumulus, cumulus, and cumulonimbus clouds. Label your picture.

9. Explain why it snows more in the mountains than it does on the plains.

10. What is another name for "frost"?

11. Explain a "front."

12. What makes thunder and lightning?

13. Do you think all hailstones fall to earth? Why or why not?

14. How do scientists track hurricanes?

15. How are tornadoes and hurricanes alike?

Water Cycle–2

TOPIC: RAIN, RAIN GO AWAY

NONFICTION: *Read About Weather* by Herta S. Breiter

FICTION: *It's Raining, It's Pouring* by Kin Eagle

Fiction: Things to Make You Think

Read the fiction book. Remember that this book is a made-up story. Choose from the activities listed below or make up your own.

1. Look carefully at the first picture. Why do the fish look so surprised? Do you think the cat is happy?

2. Name all the different containers used to catch the rain.

3. What is wrong with the old man because of the bump on his head? Why can't he wake up?

4. He finally does wake up and the rain stops. What is the weather like now?

5. What force number is the old man's sneeze, according to the nonfiction book?

6. What nursery rhyme does the picture with the cow remind you of?

7. Look in the window. Why is the old man growing? How is the old woman helping him to grow?

8. Name all the different kinds of food you see in the picture.

9. What is the old man going to do with the ladder?

10. Can you tell whether it is warm or cold? Explain the evidence.

11. What kind of weather is shown with the picture of the well?

12. Why does the weather change?

13. If the cat could talk, what do you think it would say to the old man?

14. How is the picnic broken up?

15. There is something missing in the last picture. What is it? What has happened?

RAIN, RAIN GO AWAY

Directions: Circle the activities that could be done on rainy days. Cross out the activities that would be better done on a sunny day.

Snow

Cycles of Nature–2

TOPIC: SNOW

NONFICTION: *Snow Is Falling* by Franklyn M. Branley

FICTION: *The Snowy Day* by Ezra Jack Keats

Nonfiction: Things to Make You Think

Read the nonfiction book. Remember that this is a true book and it is important to listen for the facts. Choose from the activities listed below or make up your own.

1. What makes snowflakes?

2. Are all snowflakes alike?

3. Why are some snowfalls heavy and sticky and others light, dry, and fluffy?

4. List some ways snow is good.

5. List some ways snow is bad.

6. Try the experiment in the book.

7. How can you help birds in winter?

8. Why do you think igloos keep Eskimos warm when they are out on their hunting trips?

9. How do floods happen in the spring?

10. What do you do when it snows?

11. What do your parents think about snow?

12. Use cotton balls to make a snow picture.

13. Where in the world does it snow the most?

14. Can you always find snow somewhere on Earth any time of the year?

Cycles of Nature–2

TOPIC: SNOW

NONFICTION: *Snow Is Falling* by Franklyn M. Branley

FICTION: *The Snowy Day* by Ezra Jack Keats

Fiction: Things to Make You Think

Read the fiction book. Remember that this book is a made-up story. Choose from the activities listed below or make up your own.

1. What is the little boy's name? How old do you think he is?

2. Why does the boy need a snowsuit?

3. Do you think this kind of snowfall would be a problem for cars?

4. Why do you think the snow goes "crunch"?

5. What makes all the tracks in the snow?

6. What does Peter "smack"? Why?

7. What goes "plop" on Peter's head?

8. Why doesn't Peter join the snowball fight?

9. What are some of the things Peter does in the snow?

10. What does Peter put in his pocket?

11. Why isn't the snowball in Peter's pocket after he has his bath?

12. Peter is sad when he thinks all the snow is gone. What makes him happy again?

13. The author, Ezra Jack Keats, used cut cloth to make the pictures in the book. This method is called collage. Use scraps of material, colored paper, newspaper, old wallpaper, etc., to make a picture.

14. Create a snow creature no one has ever seen before. You might use cotton balls and glue, or you might cut out a white paper figure.

SNOW

Directions: List things you can do with snow. Begin each one with a letter from the word "snowball."

S _____

N _____

O _____

W _____

B _____

A _____

L _____

L _____

Sun and Seasons

Cycles of Nature–2

TOPIC: SUN AND SEASONS
NONFICTION: *Sunshine Makes the Seasons* by Franklyn M. Branley
FICTION: *Four Stories for Four Seasons* by Tomie dePaola

Nonfiction: Things to Make You Think

Read the nonfiction book. Remember that this is a true book and it is important to listen for the facts. Choose from the activities listed below or make up your own.

1. What would happen if there were no sun?

2. How long does it take the Earth to travel around the sun?

3. Which season of the year has the longest days?

4. Why are the days warmer in summer?

5. Why don't we on Earth get dizzy going around the sun and turning every 24 hours?

6. What is the top of the Earth called?

7. What is the line around the largest part of the Earth called?

8. Try the experiment in the book.

9. Why do we have some short days and some long days?

10. Does the whole world have the same seasons at the same time?

11. Are there places on Earth that have no night or no day?

12. Where would you live if you did not like winter?

13. Name the seasons of the year.

14. Which one do you like best?

Cycles of Nature–2

TOPIC: SUN AND SEASONS
NONFICTION: *Sunshine Makes the Seasons* by Franklyn M. Branley
FICTION: *Four Stories for Four Seasons* by Tomie dePaola

Fiction: Things to Make You Think

Read the fiction book. Remember that this book is a made-up story. Choose from the activities listed below or make up your own.

1. Name the four animals that go for a stroll.

2. What are two of the animals doing that is dangerous to do in a boat?

3. Which animal thinks rowing is fun?

4. What do the four friends decide to do in summer?

5. What do they have to do to make the garden grow?

6. What kind of garden does Missy Cat have?

7. What kind of garden does Mister Frog have?

8. What kind of garden does Mistress Pig have?

9. Why is Master Dog's garden different from the others?

10. Why does Mistress Pig ask everyone to dinner?

11. How does Mistress Pig live up to her name?

12. Where do they go after Mistress Pig eats the whole dinner?

13. Why do you think Mister Frog sleeps all winter?

14. What holiday does Mister Frog always miss? Why?

15. Why can't Mister Frog find a Christmas tree?

16. How do you know the four friends are really good friends?

SUN AND SEASONS

Directions: For each of the four seasons, draw a picture of something you like to do during that season.

Winter   Spring

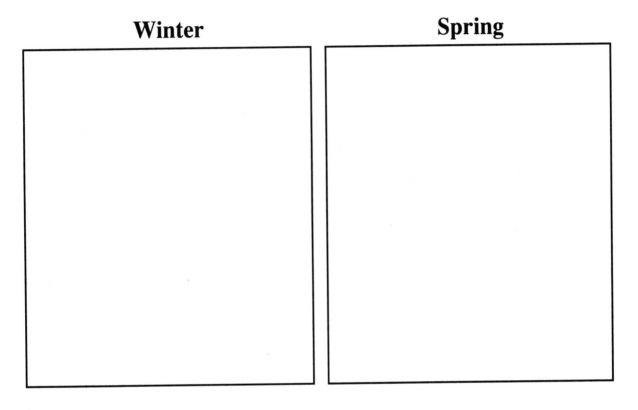

Summer   Fall

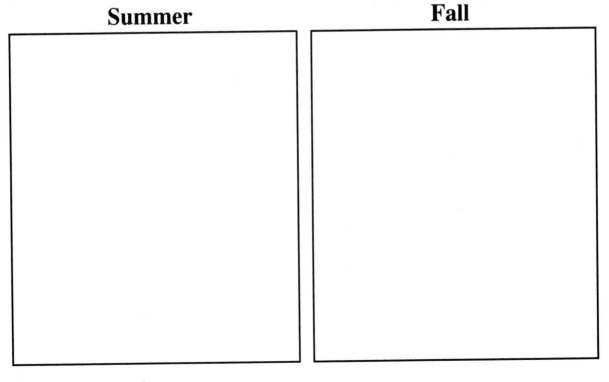

Tadpole to Frog

Life Cycles-2

TOPIC: TADPOLE TO FROG
NONFICTION: *Tale of a Tadpole* by Karen Wallace
FICTION: *Frog and Toad All Year* by Arnold Lobel

Nonfiction: Things to Make You Think

Read the nonfiction book. Remember that this is a true book and it is important to listen for the facts. Choose from the activities listed below or make up your own.

1. Where does this story begin?

2. Who lays the eggs?

3. How do the eggs stay safe in the water?

4. What is happening inside each circle of jelly?

5. How do the tadpoles get out of the jelly?

6. How do tadpoles breathe?

7. How do tadpoles escape from their enemies?

8. What happens to the tadpole that helps it swim faster?

9. What happens to the tadpole's tail?

10. Does the tadpole still breathe through gills after it loses its tail?

11. Why does the frog need to go back into the pond?

12. How does the frog catch flies? Can you do that? Why or why not?

13. What do you see under the lily pad?

14. Tell how the information in this book is like a circle.

15. Tell the steps of a frog egg that turns into a tadpole and then a full-grown frog.

Life Cycles–2

TOPIC: TADPOLE TO FROG
NONFICTION: *Tale of a Tadpole* by Karen Wallace
FICTION: *Frog and Toad All Year* by Arnold Lobel

Fiction: Things to Make You Think

Read the fiction book. Remember that this book is a made-up story. Choose from the activities listed below or make up your own.

1. How many chapters are in this book?

2. Why doesn't Toad want to go outside?

3. How does Frog get Toad ready?

4. How does Toad find out he is all alone?

5. Does Frog change Toad's mind about winter?

6. What does Frog find around the first corner in chapter 2?

7. What does Frog find around the next corner?

8. What does Frog find around the next corner after that?

9. What does Frog find around the corner of his house?

10. What time of year is it in the chapter titled "Ice Cream"?

11. Why does the ice cream melt?

12. Why are mouse, squirrel, and rabbit running away?

13. How do Frog and Toad solve the problem of the melting ice cream cones?

14. Why are Frog and Toad happy when they go to bed after raking leaves?

15. Toad is very worried about Frog. Why?

16. What kind of friends are Frog and Toad? Do you have a friend like that?

TADPOLE TO FROG

Directions: Draw pictures to go with each stage of the life cycle of a frog.

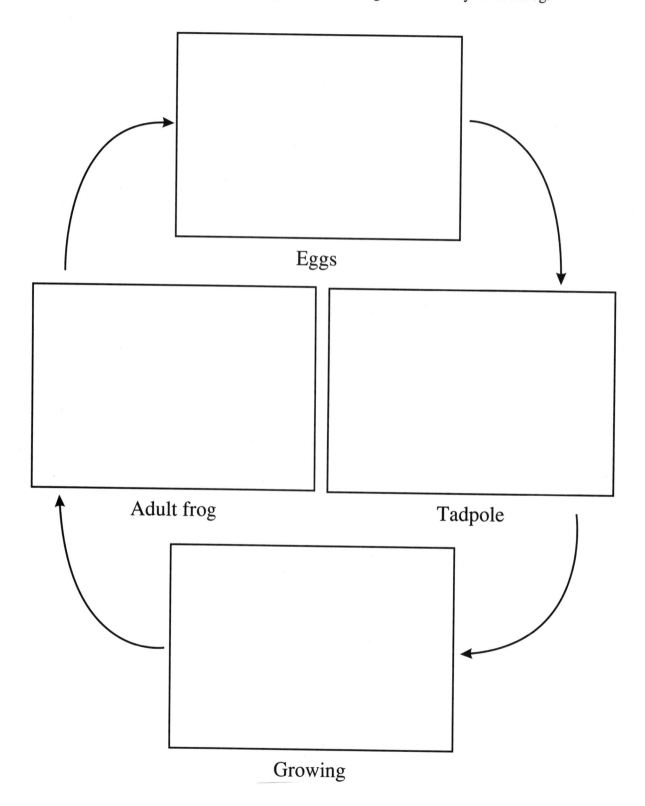

Eggs

Adult frog

Tadpole

Growing

Teeth

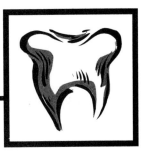

Human Body, Digestive System–2

TOPIC: TEETH
NONFICTION: *How Many Teeth?* by Paul Showers
FICTION: *Dr. De Soto* by William Steig

Nonfiction: Things to Make You Think

Read the nonfiction book. Remember that this is a true book and it is important to listen for the facts. Choose from the activities listed below or make up your own.

1. Do babies need teeth?

2. Why do you think we do not have all 32 teeth when we are children?

3. Why do you think we lose our baby teeth?

4. How do babies eat if they do not have teeth?

5. How many teeth does a one-year-old have?

6. Is it important to brush baby teeth since we lose them anyway? Why or why not?

7. How many teeth does Sam have? How may do you have?

8. Why do we need different kinds of teeth?

9. Why do our teeth get loose?

10. What is floss? Why is it important?

11. Why do you need to go to the dentist every six months?

12. Do we need our teeth to speak clearly?

Human Body, Digestive System–2

TOPIC: TEETH
NONFICTION: *How Many Teeth?* by Paul Showers
FICTION: *Dr. De Soto* by William Steig

Fiction: Things to Make You Think

Read the fiction book. Remember that this book is a made-up story. Choose from the activities listed below or make up your own.

1. Why won't Dr. De Soto treat cats?

2. Why do big animals like to go to Dr. De Soto?

3. What other animals would be dangerous to a mouse?

4. What does Dr. De Soto have to do before he can look in the fox's mouth? Why?

5. How is Dr. De Soto being brave? Is Mrs. De Soto worried? How do you know?

6. Why does Dr. De Soto put the fox to sleep?

7. What is the fox thinking of doing as he leaves the dentist's office?

8. Why is the tooth heavy for Mrs. De Soto?

9. How do the De Sotos keep the fox from eating them?

10. Hold your teeth together and recite the "Pledge of Allegiance." How does it sound?

11. Find some examples of teamwork between Dr. De Soto and his wife. Write or draw a picture to illustrate teamwork.

12. What is the meaning of the phrase "outfoxed the fox" on the very last page?

TEETH

Directions: Place the name of each tooth on the lines. Use the book to help you.

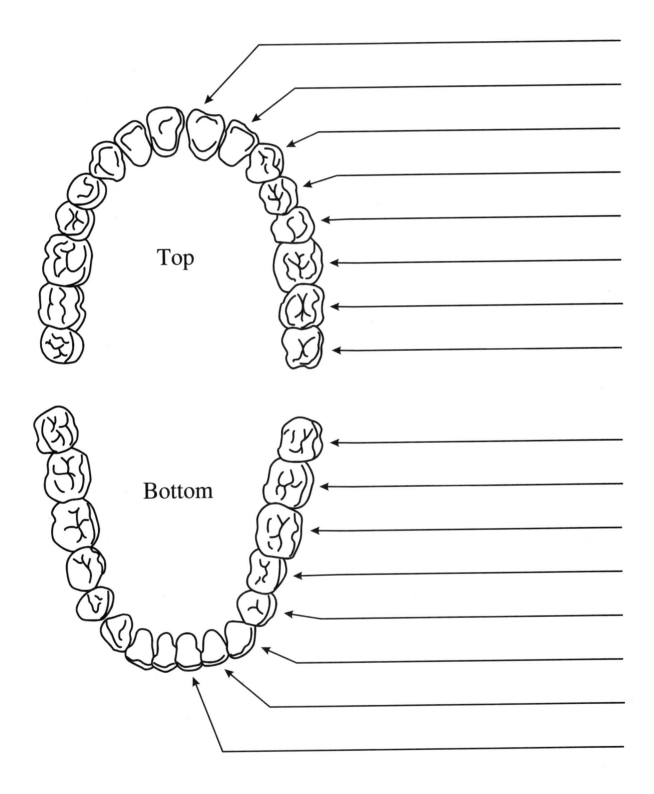

Grade

Animals

Animal Classification–3

TOPIC: ANIMALS
NONFICTION: *How to Be a Nature Detective* by Millicent E. Selsam
FICTION: *Wild Critters* by Tim Jones

Nonfiction: Things to Make You Think

Read the nonfiction book. Remember that this is a true book and it is important to listen for the facts. Choose from the activities below or make up your own.

1. What does a nature detective want to know?

2. Where can you find clues to questions about nature?

3. Why can you see all the prints from the rabbit and not all the prints from the fox?

4. How can you tell which way the animal is going?

5. Does the fox catch the rabbit in the book? How do you know?

6. Go for a walk. Look for footprints or tracks made by animals or even people's shoes. Take a picture if you have a camera, or draw them.

7. Why is it so easy to see the tracks near the river?

8. If you are near the ocean, the tracks would be made in the _____.

9. How can you tell which way the wind is coming from by watching a bird?

10. List the mammals mentioned in the book.

11. List the insects mentioned in the book.

12. List the birds mentioned in the book.

13. List the sea animals mentioned in the book.

14. Make a Detective Booklet. Begin by tracing the tracks in the book and labeling them. When you discover new tracks, draw them in your booklet or take a picture and try to label them. You may need to use books in the library to identify the tracks.

Animal Classification-3

TOPIC: ANIMALS
NONFICTION: *How to Be a Nature Detective* by Millicent E. Selsam
FICTION: *Wild Critters* by Tim Jones

Fiction: Things to Make You Think

Read the fiction book. Remember that this book is a collection of made-up poems. Choose from the activities listed below or make up your own.

1. Why don't the geese want to be found?

2. What kind of animal is yawning?

3. What kind of duck is stuck in the muck?

4. How is the baby loon like a small child?

5. What happens to the ptarmigan in winter and summer?

6. Why is the forest a dangerous place for the white moose?

7. How does the otter help the snow crab?

8. Why is the polar bear so comfortable sleeping on the ice?

9. Do you think the musk ox would like to live in New York City?

10. What is the grizzly bear doing, according to the poem?

11. What is another name for the ermine?

12. Memorize a poem of your choice.

13. Pick an animal and write your own poem about it.

14. Find three new words. Look them up in the dictionary and write the definition. You are now a dictionary detective.

Birds

Birds-3

TOPIC: BIRDS
NONFICTION: *Urban Roosts: Where Birds Nest in the City* by Barbara Bash
FICTION: *The Bird House* by Cynthia Rylant

Nonfiction: Things to Make You Think

Read the nonfiction book. Remember that this is a true book and it is important to listen for the facts. Choose from the activities listed below or make up your own.

1. What is another word for "urban"?

2. Has the pigeon always lived in the city?

3. Tell about an interesting roost where you have seen a bird.

4. What is a "clutch"?

5. Where would you look on a building to find a "cavity nester"?

6. Name other places where you might see finches and sparrows.

7. The wren uses many interesting things to pad its nest. Name five.

8. Why are barn owls able to fly at night?

9. Which birds in the book do not build nests?

10. What does the barn swallow use to make its "cup" nest?

11. How do chimney swifts hold on to the sides of the chimney?

12. What two birds in the book stay together in large groups?

13. Airports are a favorite winter home for which bird?

14. Which bird dives at speeds over 50 miles an hour?

15. The pictures of birds in this book are beautiful. Pick your favorite and draw a picture of it.

Birds–3

TOPIC: BIRDS

NONFICTION: *Urban Roosts: Where Birds Nest in the City* by Barbara Bash

FICTION: *The Bird House* by Cynthia Rylant

Fiction: Things to Make You Think

Read the fiction book. Remember that this book is a made-up story. Choose from the activities listed below or make up your own.

1. Count the birds in the picture on the first page.

2. Why do you think birds love the house?

3. Do you think the birds are afraid of the old woman?

4. Why do you think the girl runs when the birds spell "GIRL"?

5. Why do you think the owl is the one that stays quiet and then finally catches the girl?

6. Are any birds in this story also mentioned in *Urban Roosts*?

7. Can you name all the birds in this book?

8. Pick a bird and do more research on it in the library.

9. How are the birds in this story like pets?

10. If you pay attention to nature, what kinds of lessons might you learn?

11. Go outside or look out the window and draw a nature picture.

12. Nature provides shelter for the girl. How?

13. Look at the picture of the girl next to the cave at night. Can you make up a story about why she is there and what might happen to her?

14. Pretend the house is empty and no one lives there. How might the story be different?

BIRDS

Directions: On the line under each picture write FICTION if the bird would be found in a fiction book. Write NONFICTION if the bird would be found in a true book about birds.

Day and Night

Astronomy–3

TOPIC: DAY AND NIGHT
NONFICTION: *What Makes Day and Night?* by Franklyn M. Branley
FICTION: *Flashlight* by Betsy James

Nonfiction: Things to Make You Think

Read the nonfiction book. Remember that this is a true book and it is important to listen for the facts. Choose from the activities below or make up your own.

1. What is the name of our planet?

2. Why don't we feel the Earth moving?

3. Which spacecraft took the picture of the Earth from outer space?

4. How long does it take the Earth to spin around one time?

5. What makes day and night?

6. Study the pictures with the people traveling around the globe. Retell in your own words what their day is like.

7. Try the experiment. What did you learn?

8. How fast does the Earth turn?

9. Does the sun move across the sky? Why does it seem that it does?

10. What are you doing at sunrise on a regular school day?

11. What are you doing at noon on a regular school day?

12. What are you doing at sunset on a regular school day?

13. How would day and night be different if you lived on the moon?

14. About how many hours of daylight do we have each day?

15. Is that the same all over the world, and for all seasons?

Astronomy–3

TOPIC: DAY AND NIGHT
NONFICTION: *What Makes Day and Night?* by Franklyn M. Branley
FICTION: *Flashlight* by Betsy James

Fiction: Things to Make You Think

Read the fiction book. Remember that this is a made-up story. Choose from the activities listed below or make up your own.

1. The little girl is having trouble going to sleep. Why?

2. How is this house different from hers?

3. Why do you think the little sister can sleep anywhere?

4. What does she imagine the door to be?

5. Why does Grandpa come into the room?

6. What does Grandpa give the little girl?

7. Look at the picture of the table and chairs. What does your imagination see?

8. What do the shadows do when the little girl turns on the flashlight?

9. How is the flashlight like the sun? How is it different?

10. Which do you think is scarier, complete darkness or a little light that makes shadows? Try it for yourself with a flashlight and decide.

11. Why have all the bugs gathered on the screen?

12. Why does the little girl's hand glow?

13. Does she really see bears in the room? Is she having fun?

14. Why is Marie the queen of the night world?

15. Nighttime and sleep are very important. List some reasons why.

DAY AND NIGHT

Directions: Find the following words in the word search. Circle the daytime words in red and circle the nighttime words in blue.

sun   dusk   twilight   stars   moon   day
night   cloudy   light   bright   dark   dim

```
D  A  Y  D  H  T  C  I  T  D
O  J  Y  K  D  W  N  C  A  A
A  Q  Z  C  S  I  R  L  G  R
R  Y  N  M  U  L  M  O  I  K
D  G  R  D  N  I  E  U  L  M
A  B  V  C  L  G  U  D  J  O
Y  D  U  S  K  H  L  Y  I  O
U  H  G  T  F  T  Q  A  S  N
C  B  R  I  G  H  T  C  X  B
N  M  S  T  A  R  S  O  W  F
W  K  I  O  N  I  G  H  T  D
```

Ecology

Ecology-3

TOPIC: ECOLOGY
NONFICTION: *You're Aboard Spaceship Earth* by Patricia Lauber
FICTION: *Why the Sky Is Far Away* retold by Mary-Joan Gerson

Nonfiction: Things to Make You Think

Read the nonfiction book. Remember that this is a true book and it is important to listen for the facts. Choose from the activities listed below or make up your own.

1. How is the Earth like a spaceship?

2. How many miles does it travel every day?

3. How fast are we traveling on Spaceship Earth?

4. How is it possible for some of the same water that fell on the dinosaurs to also fall on you?

5. Do plants "breathe" oxygen?

6. Why doesn't the Earth run out of oxygen?

7. Plants and animals need minerals. Do you?

8. How is dead matter helpful to Spaceship Earth?

9. Explain how minerals are recycled.

10. What do you think would happen if farmers never fertilized their fields?

11. What is compost?

12. Draw a large circle with arrows to show the water cycle. Label all the important things that make the cycle work.

13. How can we keep Spaceship Earth clean and green?

14. What do you do at your house to keep Spaceship Earth clean?

Ecology–3

TOPIC: ECOLOGY
NONFICTION: *You're Aboard Spaceship Earth* by Patricia Lauber
FICTION: *Why the Sky Is Far Away* retold by Mary-Joan Gerson

Fiction: Things to Make You Think

Read the fiction book. Remember that this book is a made-up story. Choose from the activities listed below or make up your own.

1. What did the people of Nigeria long ago do with their time since they did not have to grow or hunt food?

2. Why didn't the people have to work?

3. Who is Oba?

4. Why is the sky angry?

5. The sky warns Oba about wasting the sky. What does Oba do?

6. Oba is watching the people very carefully during the festival. Why?

7. How would you describe Adese?

8. Why does Adese take more sky?

9. Do her husband and children help her eat the sky?

10. What happens when Adese buries the leftover sky?

11. Why do thunder and lightning strike?

12. Why does the sky move far away?

13. What can the people do when the sky is no longer there to feed them?

14. This book won an award for the best illustrations in a children's book. Do you like the pictures? Why or why not?

15. Folk tales and legends were told to explain or teach a lesson. What is this story trying to teach us?

Fish

Introduction to Classification of Animals-3

TOPIC: FISH

NONFICTION: *What's It Like to Be a Fish?* by Wendy Pfeffer

FICTION: *Swimmy* by Leo Leonni

Nonfiction: Things to Make You Think

Read the nonfiction book. Remember that this is a true book and it is important to listen for the facts. Choose from the activities below or make up your own.

1. Name some places where fish live.

2. What helps the fish glide through the water?

3. What helps keep a fish healthy? What helps keep you healthy?

4. How do the tail fins help the fish swim?

5. Why do fish look as if they are always drinking water?

6. Explain how fish breathe. Explain how humans breathe. Compare the two ways.

7. Explain the food chain of fish.

8. Are you warm blooded or cold blooded?

9. What temperature do fish like?

10. What temperature are humans when they are healthy?

11. Compare fish eyes and human eyes.

12. Why is it important to follow all the steps in setting up a goldfish bowl?

13. How do goldfish in a bowl get their food?

14. If you were a fish, what kind of fish would you be? Why?

Introduction to Classification of Animals–3

TOPIC: FISH

NONFICTION: *What's It Like to Be a Fish?* by Wendy Pfeffer

FICTION: *Swimmy* by Leo Leonni

Fiction: Things to Make You Think

Read the fiction book. Remember that this is a made-up story. Choose from the activities listed below or make up your own.

1. Who is the author of this story?

2. Who made the pictures?

3. What award did this book win?

4. How is Swimmy different from his brothers and sisters?

5. Which creature is the colors of the rainbow?

6. Which sea creature moves like a machine?

7. Why do you think the author calls the rocks "sugar-candy"?

8. What animal that lives on land does the eel remind you of?

9. What looks like pink palm trees?

10. Why are the red fish afraid to come out of hiding?

11. Does this story help you understand the word "teamwork"? Explain.

12. What part of the huge fish body does Swimmy become?

13. Some of the pictures look like a sponge painting. Try making an ocean picture with paints and a sponge.

14. How would you describe Swimmy? Would you want him for a friend? Why?

FISH

Directions: Finish the picture using small stars to fill in the large star just like the fish do in the book *Swimmy*.

The Moon

Astronomy, Solar System–3

TOPIC: THE MOON
NONFICTION: *The Moon Seems to Change* by Franklyn M. Branley
FICTION: *Grandfather Twilight* by Barbara Berger

Nonfiction: Things to Make You Think

Read the nonfiction book. Remember that this is a true book and it is important to listen for the facts. Choose from the activities listed below or make up your own.

1. Does the moon really change? Why does it appear that way?

2. How are the sun and the moon alike when it comes to light and dark?

3. How long is a day?

4. Is there nighttime on the moon?

5. Can you ever see the moon in the daytime?

6. Draw a picture of a crescent moon.

7. It is said that coyotes howl at what kind of moon?

8. Try the experiment with the orange. If you don't have an orange, use an old tennis ball or a rubber ball.

9. In what year did we finally see the other side of the moon?

10. Draw your own picture to show waxing and waning. Can you think of other things that wax and wane (grow and shrink in size) over and over, or expand and contract?

11. Watch the moon for a week or even a month. Draw a picture of what it looks like each night. Does it change? Name the phases.

12. Would you like to travel to the moon? Why or why not?

Astronomy, Solar System–3

TOPIC: THE MOON
NONFICTION: *The Moon Seems to Change* by Franklyn M. Branley
FICTION: *Grandfather Twilight* by Barbara Berger

Fiction: Things to Make You Think

Read the fiction book. Remember that this book is a made-up story. Choose from the activities listed below or make up your own.

1. How do you know this story is fiction?

2. Where does Grandfather Twilight live?

3. When does he close his book, comb his beard, and put on his jacket?

4. What is Grandfather Twilight carrying?

5. Where are the pearls kept?

6. How is Grandfather Twilight changing in each of the pictures?

7. What is happening to the pearl?

8. What do the animals do as Grandfather Twilight passes through the forest?

9. Where does Grandfather Twilight end his walk?

10. What does the pearl become?

11. Where does Grandfather Twilight go after he sets the moon?

12. What do we call the time between "day is done" and "bedtime"?

13. Do you think the "pearl" is always round every night?

14. What other shapes might the "pearl" be?

THE MOON

Directions: Draw a picture of the moon that shows waxing and one that shows waning.

Waxing

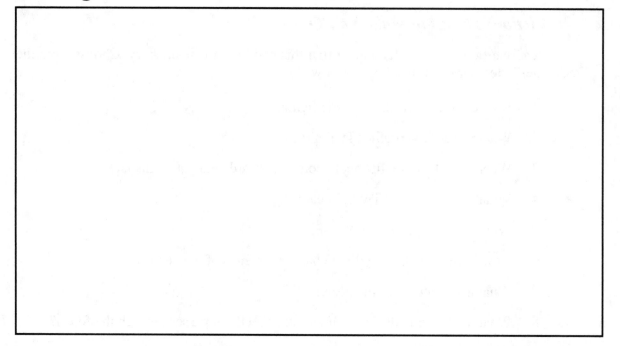

Waning

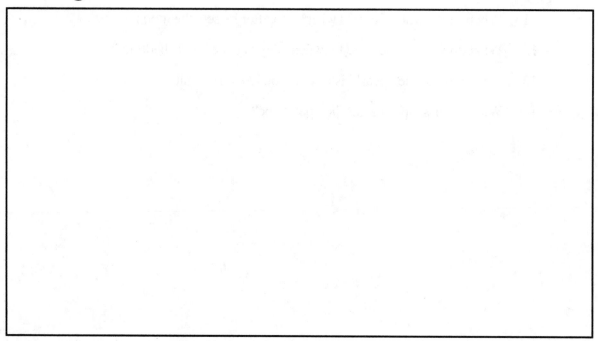

Moon Landing

Astronomy–3

TOPIC: MOON LANDING
NONFICTION: *What the Moon Is Like* by Franklyn M. Branley
FICTION: *The Unicorn and the Moon* by Tomie dePaola

Nonfiction: Things to Make You Think

Read the nonfiction book. Remember that this is a true book and it is important to listen for the facts. Choose from the activities listed below or make up your own.

1. Is there really a "man in the moon"?

2. Why do people think it looks like there is a face in the moon?

3. What are the craters?

4. Is there water on the moon? Can there be life?

5. What are some things that are the same on the moon as on Earth?

6. What are some things that are different on the moon and on Earth?

7. There were six *Apollo* moon missions, but there were supposed to be seven. What happened to *Apollo 13*?

8. The astronauts had to wear space suits while on the moon. Why?

9. Why is the moon so dull and drab?

10. What protects the Earth but not the moon from the sun?

11. How much would you weigh if you were on the moon?

12. Why didn't the astronauts want to fall down while walking on the moon?

13. Why hasn't the moon changed for billions of years?

14. What is a moonquake? How is that different from an earthquake?

15. Why is the sky blue?

Astronomy–3

TOPIC: MOON LANDING
NONFICTION: *What the Moon Is Like* by Franklyn M. Branley
FICTION: *The Unicorn and the Moon* by Tomie dePaola

Fiction: Things to Make You Think

Read the fiction book. Remember that this book is a made-up story. Choose from the activities listed below or make up your own.

1. Read the foreword before the beginning of the story.

2. Long ago people told stories to try to explain things about the universe and life that they did not understand. What is this story trying to explain?

3. Why does the unicorn seek the light of the moon?

4. How does the moon get caught between the two hills?

5. Why do the hills want to keep the moon trapped between them?

6. What does the unicorn do first to try to free the moon?

7. Why doesn't that work?

8. What does the unicorn do next to try to free the moon without hurting it?

9. Is the unicorn afraid of the terrible-looking griffin? Why or why not?

10. Is the griffin able to help? Why or why not?

11. How does the moon finally get free?

12. Who is smarter, the hills or the alchemist?

13. What does the moon promise the unicorn?

14. Why does the unicorn keep the mirrors "just in case"?

15. Tell a story about the sun getting caught and not being able to rise or set.

MOON LANDING

Directions: Using the word list, decide which words are FICTION and which are NONFICTION. Place them in the correct list.

Word List:

unicorn	crater	astronaut	griffin
gravity	moon car	trolls	man in the moon
trapped moon	talking rabbits	Jack and Jill	water on the moon

Fiction   Nonfiction

_____   _____

_____   _____

_____   _____

_____   _____

_____   _____

_____   _____

_____   _____

_____   _____

_____   _____

_____   _____

_____   _____

Oceans

Classification of Animals–3

TOPIC: OCEANS

NONFICTION: *Oceans* by Katherine Jones Carter

FICTION: *Henry & Mudge & the Forever Sea* by Cynthia Rylant

Nonfiction: Things to Make You Think

Read the nonfiction book. Remember that this is a true book and it is important to listen for the facts. Choose from the activities listed below or make up your own.

1. Are all the oceans of the world connected?

2. What is the difference between an ocean and a sea?

3. Why are some oceans blue and some green?

4. Where would you find beautiful colored fish?

5. From where do icebergs come?

6. Why does the fish need a flashlight?

7. Why are there whitecaps on the ocean on some days but not on other days?

8. Why are tides a daily happening? Use the words "ebb" and "flow" in your answer.

9. Listen to a weather report. Does the reporter mention the Gulf Stream?

10. Why is the Gulf Stream so important?

11. The ocean is full of life. Name three animals that live in warm water. Name three animals that live in cold water.

12. Why do we find so many empty seashells on the beach?

13. Name some ways the ocean helps feed us.

14. What are some other helpful things that come from the sea?

15. Have you been to the ocean? Tell or write about your experience.

Classification of Animals–3

TOPIC: OCEANS

NONFICTION: *Oceans* by Katherine Jones Carter

FICTION: *Henry & Mudge & the Forever Sea* by Cynthia Rylant

Fiction: Things to Make You Think

Read the fiction book. Remember that this book is a made-up story. Choose from the activities listed below or make up your own.

1. What kind of dog is Mudge?

2. What if Mudge did drink the salty water from the ocean? What do you think would happen?

3. Why do you think Henry's father keeps singing, "Yo, ho, ho"?

4. What makes the ocean blue and white?

5. Why is the land next to the water sand?

6. Imagine you are at the beach with Henry and Mudge. What would you be doing?

7. Why can't Henry and his father swim against the waves?

8. What do you think would happen if Mudge swam out into the ocean?

9. Which lunch would you have ordered: Henry's lunch, Henry's father's lunch, or Mudge's lunch?

10. If you were at the beach, what would you build in the sand other than a castle?

11. Why do you think Mudge goes in the ocean after the lobster when he will not go in earlier in the story?

12. Why can't Henry and his father have crab for dinner?

13. What kind of father is Henry's father? Why?

14. Give this story a new title. Make up several.

OCEANS

Directions: Find the following words in the word hunt puzzle.

blue	green	ebb	flow	whitecap
ocean	fish	gulf	seashells	sand
beach	tide	salty	crab	iceberg

```
G  U  L  F  S  A  L  T  Y  O
W  T  I  D  E  B  O  R  G  L
G  H  C  R  A  B  E  E  H  S
R  A  I  T  S  A  B  D  U  I
E  C  F  T  H  B  O  A  H  C
E  B  L  U  E  S  C  P  C  E
N  G  O  R  L  C  E  L  A  B
W  O  W  H  L  B  A  L  E  E
E  A  F  I  S  H  N  P  B  R
D  N  S  A  N  D  C  R  A  G
```

Outer Space

Astronomy–3

TOPIC: OUTER SPACE
NONFICTION: *Is There Life in Outer Space?* by Franklyn M. Branley
FICTION: *Space Invaders* by Sarah Albee

Nonfiction: Things to Make You Think

Read the nonfiction book. Remember that this is a true book and it is important to listen for the facts. Choose from the activities listed below or make up your own.

1. Does the astronomer really see creatures on the moon?

2. Why do you think people believe the stories about moon creatures and Martians?

3. Who are Neil Armstrong and Edwin Aldren?

4. In what year did human beings land on the moon?

5. Why was it important to explore the moon?

6. How did we prove there is no life on Mars without landing there?

7. How did we find out about Mercury?

8. What did we find out about Venus?

9. Can there be life on any of the other planets?

10. Could there be life outside our solar system?

11. Do we know what other forms of life might look like?

12. Where do people come up with ideas about what other life forms may look like?

13. Do you think it is "silly" to think about other life forms in outer space?

14. Would you like to explore outer space? Why or why not?

15. Scientists have discovered no life on any of the planets in our solar system. Does that mean there is no life in outer space?

Astronomy–3

TOPIC: OUTER SPACE
NONFICTION: *Is There Life in Outer Space?* by Franklyn M. Branley
FICTION: *Space Invaders* by Sarah Albee

Fiction: Things to Make You Think

Read the fiction book. Remember that this book is a made-up story. Choose from the activities listed below or make up your own.

1. What do you think Chuckie and Tommy are watching on TV?

2. Why does Chuckie hide behind a curtain?

3. What do the boys see that makes them think the space invaders are here?

4. Is Dad really going to the craft show to buy a spacecraft?

5. What is Stu doing in the basement?

6. Didi is getting ready. What does she use on her face?

7. Why do Chuckie and Tommy think Grandpa Lou is getting ready for space invaders?

8. What does Tommy's shirt have on the front?

9. What is Spike the dog actually carrying?

10. What is sitting on the picnic table?

11. Why are the babies crying?

12. Stu is an inventor. What does he invent?

13. What kind of party is going on in the backyard?

14. Tell or write about a time when you let your imagination "run away with you" as Tommy and Chuckie do.

OUTER SPACE

Directions: Use the word list to fill in the Venn diagram. If something can be found only on Earth, write it in the right-hand circle. If it can be found only in outer space, write the word it in the left-hand circle. If it can be found in both places, write the word in the middle section.

Word List:

animals	plants	rocks	dust
light	dark	people	craters
hills	water	life	stars
planets	meteors	asteroids	sun

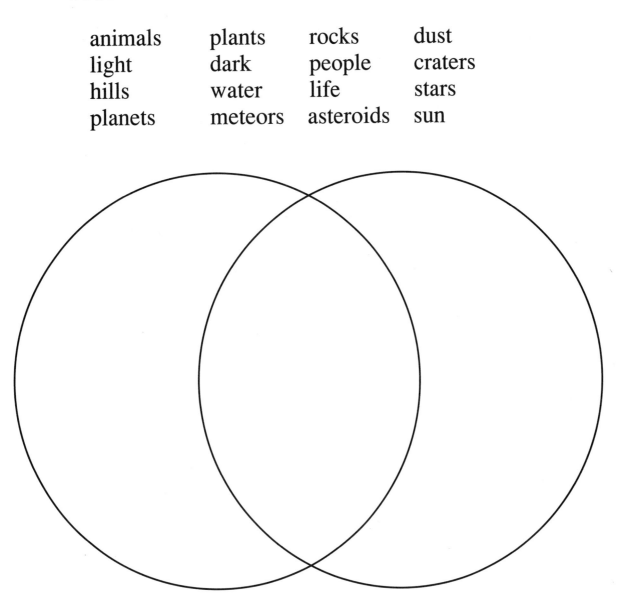

Pollution

Ecology-3

TOPIC: POLLUTION

NONFICTION: *Global Change* by Theodore P. Snow

FICTION: *The Berenstain Bears Don't Pollute (Anymore)* by Stan Berenstain and Jan Berenstain

Nonfiction: Things to Make You Think

Read the nonfiction book. Remember that this is a true book and it is important to listen for the facts. Choose from the activities listed below or make up your own.

1. The Earth began about 4.5 billion years ago. Write down that number.

2. Life appeared 3.5 billion years ago. Write down that number.

3. What layer of gases allowed life to continue to grow and survive?

4. How do plants allow humans to survive?

5. Explain how plates are a part of our changing Earth.

6. What are some of the causes of "global change"?

7. Explain the greenhouse effect.

8. In what ways is carbon dioxide released into the atmosphere? Why is this harmful?

9. What might happen due to the greenhouse effect?

10. The ozone layer protects us from what kind of light?

11. Explain what CFCs are. How are they helpful and how are they harmful?

12. What is the worst thing that can happen to the water?

13. Why are heat and rain bad for water?

14. How are habitats being destroyed? Why is this bad?

15. What do people have to do in the future to protect our Earth?

Ecology–3

TOPIC: POLLUTION

NONFICTION: *Global Change* by Theodore P. Snow

FICTION: *The Berenstain Bears Don't Pollute (Anymore)* by Stan Berenstain and Jan Berenstain

Fiction: Things to Make You Think

Read the fiction book. Remember that this book is a made-up story. Choose from the activities listed below or make up your own.

1. Do you think Professor Actual Factual is a good name for this character in the book? Why or why not? Can you think of another name?

2. Why does Papa think Bear Country is beautiful?

3. How is the animals' view of Bear Country different from Papa's view from the front porch?

4. The name Bearsonian Institution is copied from a real museum in Washington, D.C. Can you name it?

5. Who does Professor Actual Factual think is really endangered?

6. Why do you think the Professor needs an Actual Factualmobile? What kinds of instruments might be in the van?

7. Why do you think it is hard to make grown-ups help with the pollution problem?

8. Explain the meaning of the three words the Professor teaches the cubs.

9. What do you do at your house to help with the pollution problem?

10. Papa's dream helps him to take action. What does he do?

11. What can you do about pollution?

12. Find out where recycling is being done: school? church? businesses? stores?

13. Make a sign of your own to promote Earth-friendly habits.

14. Why is it important for Papa Bear to plant a tree for every one that is cut down?

POLLUTION

Directions: Make an animal book that shows an animal on one side of the page. On the other side of the page describe how pollution does or could affect that animal.

For example:

Skeletons

Human Body-3

TOPIC: SKELETONS

NONFICTION: *The Skeleton Inside You* by Philip Balestrino

FICTION: *In a Dark, Dark Room and Other Scary Stories* by Alvin Schwartz

Nonfiction: Things to Make You Think

Read the nonfiction book. Remember that this is a true book and it is important to listen for the facts. Choose from the activities listed below or make up your own.

1. Do you think your skeleton is scary? Why or why not?

2. Why can't you change your shape like a ball of clay?

3. How is a chair like your skeleton and your body?

4. How many bones are there in your body?

5. Add up the bones in your hand and arm. Is the book correct?

6. Explain the difference between bones and cartilage.

7. Feel the cartilage in your ear and end of your nose.

8. How does the doctor take a look at your bones?

9. Do bones grow like other parts of your body?

10. Are your bones a living thing?

11. Tell why calcium is so important to your bones.

12. Try to tie yourself into knots.

13. Why is bone marrow so important to our bodies?

14. How do some bones protect organs in your body?

15. How many joints do you have in your body?

16. Tell about a time when you were protected by your bones.

Human Body–3

TOPIC: SKELETONS

NONFICTION: *The Skeleton Inside You* by Philip Balestrino

FICTION: *In a Dark, Dark Room and Other Scary Stories* by Alvin Schwartz

Fiction: Things to Make You Think

Read the fiction book. Remember that this book is a made-up story. Choose from the activities listed below or make up your own.

1. Why does the author suggest that you read or tell these stories slowly and quietly?

2. In the story "The Teeth," why do you think the boy is scared? Would you be scared?

3. Why do you think the woman tries to talk to the corpses?

4. Do you think she expects to get an answer?

5. Have you ever gone on a picnic in a graveyard? Would you like to?

6. Do you know anyone who always wears something around his or her neck?

7. Do you think Jenny should have told Alfred about the green scarf earlier?

8. What is in the dark wood?

9. What is in the dark house?

10. What is in the dark room?

11. What is in the dark chest?

12. What is on the dark shelf?

13. What is in the dark box?

14. How do you think the sweater ends up on the grave?

15. Name in order the places that Ruth looks for the ghost.

16. Memorize the poem "The Ghost of John."

17. Tell one of these stories to five different people. After that, you will always remember it.

SKELETONS

Directions: Draw a picture of a skeleton. Label the major bones using the word list.

Word List:

skull	jaw	neck	collarbone	shoulder blade
backbone	tailbone	heel	knee	breastbone
toes	foot	pelvis	ribs	hand

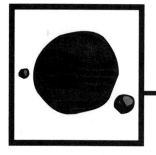

Solar System

Astronomy–3

TOPIC: SOLAR SYSTEM
NONFICTION: *The Magic School Bus Lost in the Solar System* by Joanna Cole
FICTION: *Cam Jansen and the Mystery of the U.F.O.* by David A. Adler

Nonfiction: Things to Make You Think

Read the nonfiction book. Remember that this is a true book and it is important to listen for the facts. Choose from the activities listed below or make up your own.

1. Where are the students and Ms. Friggle going on their field trip?

2. Have you ever been to a planetarium on a field trip? Tell about it or tell about another time you have viewed the stars.

3. Read the report by Wanda. How do spaceships "break free" of the Earth's gravity?

4. How does the Magic School Bus break free?

5. Why are the students floating around inside the bus?

6. Why do the kids have to wear spacesuits?

7. What are solar flares?

8. What are sun spots?

9. Why are the students heavier when they land on Venus?

10. What is the greenhouse effect?

11. What is the asteroid belt?

12. How does the bus get lost in the solar system?

13. How do the students continue learning while they are lost?

14. Name the three planets that are yellowish looking, red, and blue.

15. How does Janet save the day?

Astronomy–3

TOPIC: SOLAR SYSTEM
NONFICTION: *The Magic School Bus Lost in the Solar System* by Joanna Cole
FICTION: *Cam Jansen and the Mystery of the U.F.O.* by David A. Adler

Fiction: Things to Make You Think

Read the fiction book. Remember that this book is a made-up story. Choose from the activities listed below or make up your own.

1. What does "Cam" stand for?

2. Why does she have this nickname?

3. What kind of a contest is Eric planning to enter?

4. List the rules of the Junior News Photography Contest.

5. Cam has a photographic memory. What does this mean?

6. What grade are the kids in at school?

7. How do they get the kitten down out of the tree safely?

8. Why can't they figure out how many lights are in the sky?

9. Why do the people in the parking lot all have binoculars?

10. What does Eric take a picture of with his last picture?

11. How is Cam able to locate the tree that was brushed by the UFO?

12. Cindy and Steven are covered with tin foil to look like what?

13. Why is Bobby staging this hoax?

14. Do you think that is fair?

15. Eric's real camera is used to take a winning photo in the photography contest. How do Cam's "mental camera" and Eric's real camera make a good team?

SOLAR SYSTEM

Directions: Find the following words in the word hunt puzzle.

gravity	rockets	atmosphere	clouds
weightless	orbit	sunspots	water
vapor	space	sulfuric acid	
asteroid	craters	aliens	

```
S  N  U  C  R  A  T  E  R  S  C  D
W  E  I  G  H  T  L  E  S  S  W  T
A  I  O  V  K  M  F  L  U  S  R  C
T  L  S  C  R  O  C  K  E  T  S  S
E  A  T  R  A  S  T  E  R  O  I  D
R  R  O  K  S  P  A  C  E  R  B  U
V  O  P  E  P  H  E  G  H  B  I  O
A  P  S  A  O  E  R  O  P  I  T  L
P  C  N  R  G  R  A  V  I  T  Y  C
O  I  U  T  I  E  V  P  S  C  D  R
R  R  S  L  C  T  S  A  S  B  I  T
S  U  L  F  U  R  I  C  A  C  I  D
```

Spiders

Introduction to Animal Classification–3

TOPIC: SPIDERS

NONFICTION: *Spiders* by Gail Gibbons

FICTION: *Anansi the Spider: A Tale from the Ashanti* by Gerald McDermott

Nonfiction: Things to Make You Think

Read the nonfiction book. Remember that this is a true book and it is important to listen for the facts. Choose from the activities listed below or make up your own.

1. Do you think spiders are scary? Why or why not?

2. How many different kinds of spiders are there?

3. How small can they be?

4. How big can they grow?

5. Which animals appeared first on Earth, spiders or dinosaurs?

6. Can you retell the story of how the spider group got the name arachnid?

7. List all the ways in which a spider's body is different from an insect's body.

8. How does the male spider keep the female spider from eating him?

9. What are spiderlings?

10. Do spiderlings go ballooning just for fun? Why do they do it?

11. What happens when a spider molts?

12. Draw a picture of each of the five kinds of webs. See if you can find any.

13. Do all spiders spin webs?

14. Which spiders use camouflage to catch insects?

15. Which spiders are dangerous?

16. How do spiders help us?

Introduction to Animal Classification–3

TOPIC: SPIDERS

NONFICTION: *Spiders* by Gail Gibbons

FICTION: *Anansi the Spider: A Tale from the Ashanti* by Gerald McDermott

Fiction: Things to Make You Think

Read the fiction book. Remember that this book is a made-up story. Choose from the activities listed below or make up your own.

1. This is a tale from the Ashanti people. Where do they live?

2. How many sons does Anansi have?

3. Look at the mouth on Anansi as he leaves home, travels far away, and falls into trouble. How does the mouth change across the pages?

4. What trouble does he fall into?

5. Which son first knows his father is in trouble?

6. How does Road Builder help to find Anansi?

7. How does River Drinker help?

8. What does Game Skinner do to help Anansi?

9. What is the trouble that happened then?

10. How does Stone Thrower help Anansi escape from the Falcon?

11. Anansi wants to thank the son that rescues him by giving him a present. What is the gift to be?

12. What is Anansi's next problem?

13. Whom does Anansi ask for help?

14. What do they argue about?

15. Name places the globe in the sky. You can see it tonight. What do we call it?

Stars

Astronomy–3

TOPIC: STARS

NONFICTION: *The Sky Is Full of Stars* by Franklyn M. Branley

FICTION: *Coyote Places the Stars* by Harriet Peck Taylor

Nonfiction: Things to Make You Think

Read the nonfiction book. Remember that this is a true book and it is important to listen for the facts. Choose from the activities listed below or make up some of your own.

1. Where are the stars?

2. Can you see all the stars that are in the sky?

3. How are the stars different?

4. Why do the stars seem to rise and set like the sun?

5. Can you see the same stars in the winter sky that you see in the summer?

6. What is another name for star pictures?

7. What is a constellation? How many are there?

8. The Big Dipper is a part of what bigger constellation?

9. What is the brightest constellation in the winter sky?

10. List the nine stars mentioned in the book.

11. What do scientists use to study the stars?

12. Follow the directions on how to make your own constellations. You can find more information and pictures of constellations in books at the library.

13. Stargazing can be enjoyed all your life and anywhere you travel or live. Where would you like to live or travel?

Astronomy–3

TOPIC: STARS
NONFICTION: _The Sky Is Full of Stars_ by Franklyn M. Branley
FICTION: _Coyote Places the Stars_ by Harriet Peck Taylor

Fiction: Things to Make You Think

Read the fiction book. Remember that this book is a made-up story. Choose from the activities listed below or make up your own.

1. How does Coyote make a ladder to the moon?

2. Why is Coyote happy when he discovers he can move the stars around?

3. Name all of coyote's friends who are made into star pictures.

4. Why does coyote begin to howl?

5. Name the animals that follow Coyote's voice.

6. Are the animals pleased with Coyote's handiwork?

7. When you hear a coyote howl, what are you supposed to do?

8. What are legends, and why do you think they are told?

9. If you could create a constellation, what would you create, and how would you reach the sky to arrange the stars?

10. Try to draw an animal in the style of the illustrator. At the end of the story you can read how the illustrator created all the pictures for the book.

11. Which animal is your favorite?

12. What do you think the animals would do at a party?

Waterways

Ecology, Rivers–3

TOPIC: WATERWAYS
NONFICTION: *Follow the Water from Brook to Ocean* by Arthur Dorros
FICTION: *Bill and Pete Go Down the Nile* by Tomie dePaola

Nonfiction: Things to Make You Think

Read the nonfiction book. Remember that this is a true book and it is important to listen for the facts. Choose from the activities below or make up some of your own.

1. Water always flows.

2. Where does water collect?

3. The lowest places on Earth are the _____.

4. Does all water flow to the ocean?

5. A brook flows into a _____.

6. Can you canoe in a brook?

7. What is erosion?

8. What river carved out the Grand Canyon?

9. What makes a river move faster?

10. Why are some rivers muddy-looking?

11. What makes electricity at a dam?

12. A delta is at the _____ of the river.

13. Using a map or an atlas, find the following rivers:

    a. Mississippi River

    b. Missouri River

    c. Arkansas River

    d. Colorado River

    List some smaller rivers or streams that flow into these rivers.

14. Floods cause a great deal of damage. How do we try to control floods?

Ecology, Rivers–3

TOPIC: WATERWAYS
NONFICTION: *Follow the Water from Brook to Ocean* by Arthur Dorros
FICTION: *Bill and Pete Go Down the Nile* by Tomie dePaola

Fiction: Things to Make You Think

Read the fiction book. Remember that this is a made up-story. Choose from the activities listed below or make up your own.

1. Bill and Pete are friends. Why?

2. What makes a good friend? How do you want your good friends to treat you?

3. Locate the country of Egypt on a world map. Are there any other important rivers in Egypt?

4. What cities are located along the Nile?

5. What is William Everett Crocodile's nickname?

6. What is Bill's hometown?

7. What is Pete's important job?

8. Why do all the crocodiles have birds on their backs?

9. Where does the class go on their class trip?

10. How does Pete save Bill?

11. How does the class get home?

12. Look up the word "symbiosis." Do Bill and Pete have a symbiotic relationship?

13. Would you like to visit Egypt? Why or why not?

14. Write a story about your adventure on a trip down the Nile. Compare your adventure to Bill's and Pete's.

WATERWAYS

Directions: Draw a picture of a brook, stream, river, and ocean, showing the difference in their sizes.

Brook

Stream

River

Ocean

Author/Title/Subject Index

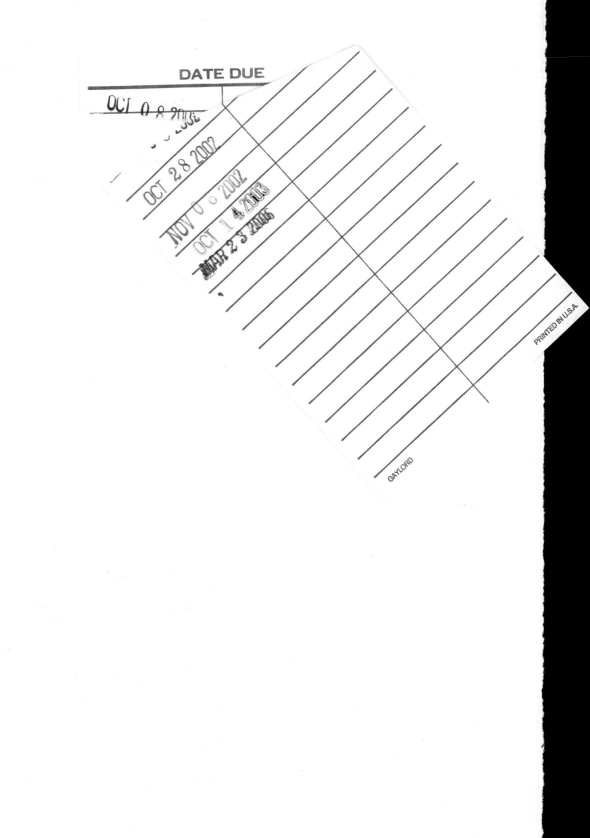